WASTED VALOR

The Confederate Dead at Gettysburg

by Gregory A. Coco

Foreword by Dr. William H. Ridinger, Ed.D.

Maps by Daniel E. Fuhrman

Sketches by John S. Heiser

Design and layout by Dean S. Thomas

Printed and bound in the United States of America

Published by THOMAS PUBLICATIONS, Gettysburg, Pa. 17325

Library of Congress Catalog Card Number: 89-051932

ISBN-0-939631-22-9

Dedication

In remembrance of Private Octave Mayeux, 2nd Louisiana Infantry, a resident of Avoyelles Parish, Louisiana, and the many thousands like him who rotted into dust in the rich Pennsylvania earth, nevermore to embrace the pleasures of home, family and friends.

Contents

FOREWORD

What happened to the Confederate dead? If this question was asked once of me during my many years at Gettysburg, it was surely asked hundreds of times by visitors, especially as they walked through the Soldiers' National Cemetery. When told about the sad fate of most of the Confederate dead, and how they were carelessly buried with little or no attempt at identification by Union soldiers, almost all visitors, regardless where they hail from, are shocked by this information. Quite a few people cannot understand why the cemetery does not include all of the Confederate burials (a few *were* mistakenly buried in it), and wonder why these men, Americans all, were not properly interred with identification and headstones. Of course most people do not realize that at first even the Union soldiers had only crude headboards to mark their graves while only Southerners buried by their comrades were likely to have the same.

Usually the strongest reaction, besides that of anguish and sadness expressed by visitors, comes when they are informed that most of the Confederate bodies were left in their makeshift graves for nine to ten years after the battle. Then mainly through the efforts of several patriotic organizations some money was eventually raised to pay for the exhuming, boxing, shipment south, and eventual reburial of the remains in Confederate cemeteries in Richmond, Virginia, Raleigh, North Carolina, Charleston, South Carolina, and Savannah, Georgia, identified in each place with a tablet indicating only two words: *Gettysburg Dead.* It is my experience that this fact does more than the most vivid and dramatic accounts of the desperate and savage fighting that occurred in such places as the Wheatfield, Devil's Den, and during Pickett's charge to underscore the tragic futility of war. This realization causes many for the first time to understand the terrible cost of war in terms of human values and the traumatic damage done the human soul.

Upon further reflection while reading this book, I remembered some experiences from my young boyhood in Gettysburg during the 1920s, of stories told by old vets and their younger relatives about southern people coming to the Battlefield to either find the place where a relative fell or where that person was buried. I dimly remember the reverent sadness that prevailed along with happy recollections of the young soldier's earlier years when seemingly his life held so much promise. On at least one occasion the visitor scooped earth into a paper bag and a number of them even took

7

photographs of the scene. In that long ago time I was too young and innocent to understand or appreciate; now I do all too well.

For me and I think for numerous others, the shabby treatment of the Confederate dead by elements of the Union army while understandable given the time and circumstances, was deplorable. Of course the burial squads were not to blame as they had little time and were engaged in work of a most horrible and sickening nature. And given the hatred that prevailed throughout the country which infected most people, the wonder is that the burials were done as well as they were. General Meade, the victor of Gettysburg, speaking at the laying of the cornerstone for the Soldiers' National monument in July of 1865, expressed regrets that the Confederate dead were not buried appropriately in land nearby. He was severely criticized for his compassion and concern for his former enemies.

Wasted Valor, on one hand, is a very appropriate and fitting title for this book. Many times in war valor (courage) is not enough; and all too often it is expended in unjustified wars. Unfortunately it is the soldiers' duty "Not to wonder why; but only to do or die." Confederates killed or mortally wounded at Gettysburg, brought so forcibly to our attention by Gregory Coco, were fighting for what they believed right, most not for slavery, but for independence from a Union that seemed to threaten rights guaranteed by the Constitution and other values they cherished.

Yet, on the other hand, was their valor wasted? If so, then their deaths were doubly tragic with no redemption at all. Most Southerners wanted to be free from Northern dominance and control. Their thinking and feelings were very much like that of the Founding Fathers who revolted against England in the name of liberty and independence. Most of the men of the South, just as many men of the American colonies, were willing to risk death for what they believed right. We respect, revere, and honor those who fought and died for American independence. Yet in the North after the Civil War, and today throughout a large part of the country, Confederate casualties are forgotten by most. For me, their valor was not wasted because they fought and died for a cause they believed right; and I know that a feeling such as this is a basic American belief valued and appreciated by most people.

Throughout the book, Gregory Coco shows an emotional and spiritual bond with fighting men; very likely because of his own traumatic combat experiences in Vietnam. His section of fifty biographies of Confederates who died at Gettysburg is exceptionally dramatic and compelling as he recounts the last words and feelings expressed by those on the verge of death. He also gives you eyewitness accounts, when available, of a number of burials which immerses one in scenes of despair and sadness that robs war of its glamour and glory. Through painstaking research, Coco has personalized these dead men to the extent that I felt that I was there and was strongly affected by what I had seen and heard.

While there are several recent books that deal with the casualties of both Civil War armies at Gettysburg, there is none to my knowledge that so thoroughly covers every aspect of the fate of the deceased soldiers as does this book. Here, for the first time, is a complete history of the treatment of the dead, from their battlefield deaths and early descriptions of the corpse-strewn field, to hasty burials, to visitors drawn out of curiosity, relatives seeking loved ones, early disinterments, the mapping and listing the locations of the Confederate graves ending with the contracted removal of these soldiers and the shipment of their remains to major Southern cities.

From my personal experience at Gettysburg, I have no doubt that this book will have great appeal to many Southerners due to their strong family values and ties, not to mention the fact that the "Lost Cause" is still very much a force in Southern culture. Furthermore, I believe that because of the fascination the Civil War has for hundreds of thousands of Americans, especially the historians, students, scholars, and "buffs," that Coco will have a viable market for his book. The "bottom line" for me, relative to this work, is Coco's forceful and poignant portrayal of the aftermath of battle and the terrible human costs of war. I am convinced that no study of the war is complete until the story of the dead is told and Coco has very effectively accomplished that here.

Perhaps only one other has said it better than the author, and that was Theodore O'Hara who, 143 years ago, honored the American dead of the Mexican War with these lines:

The muffled drum's sad roll has beat
the soldier's last tattoo;
No more on life's parade shall meet
that brave and fallen few.
On Fame's eternal camping ground
their silent tents are spread,
And glory guards, with solemn round,
the bivouac of the dead.

Gregory Coco, through this book, does much to underscore that "glory guards, with solemn round, the bivouac of the [Confederate] dead." Despite his title *Wasted Valor*, sensitive and knowledgeable people, because of his powerful and gripping portrayal of events, may conclude that these Confederates did not die in vain at Gettysburg - that their lives were given in a cause they believed right, just as did their Union brothers who set the stage for the birth of a true and stronger nation. Although they did not live to see it, their valor has contributed to the making of present day America.

Dr. William Ridinger
March 13, 1990

Acknowledgements

A book on this subject could not have been realized without using earlier works of other historians. The most important research tools at my disposal were Kathleen Georg Harrison's detailed rosters of the known Confederate dead, which she compiled from the handbook and burial lists of Dr. John W.C. O'Neal, J.G. Frey, the Weaver family and others. By now, it must be all too apparent that I am unable to successfully complete a project without the assistance and direction of my dear friend Kathy Harrison; therefore I most heartily thank her for these continued kindnesses. Several other people are also very high on my list to acknowledge. They are Robert K. Krick, John W. Busey, Edward F. Guy, Roy E. Frampton, Paul M. Shevchuk, John S. Heiser, Dr. William Ridinger, William A. Frassanito, and Dr. Charles H. Glatfelter. By their excellent research abilities and published works, all added much to the store of knowledge available on the subject of Confederate deaths. For instance, Bob Krick's *Confederate Death Roster* was so often referred to that for weeks it never left my side.

My deep appreciation, love and thanks also go out to Cindy L. Small for her word processing and editing skills, and for the many hours spent patiently accommodating my horrible penmanship, misspellings, and unannounced changes. Any success with this publication may be mostly attributed to her.

A special acknowledgement must go out to Daniel E. Fuhrman for his professional cartography. Despite the birth of his first baby (Bryce Daniel) while returning to college and holding down a full-time job, somehow, Dan eagerly accepted my invitation to lend his skills to this undertaking.

Finally, I would like to thank my friends, Jeane and Dean Thomas for their faith in this book and their growing publishing experience which finalized this project, and Jim Thomas for his "behind the scenes" skills so necessary to the mechanical end of the publishing process.

All of you are irreplaceable as friends and will always be in my memory, as I am forever obligated to you.

Introduction

The one great drawback to a visit to the field of Gettysburg is that it haunts one. Dreams, sometimes realistic, sometimes most grotesque, are apt for weeks to invade the slumbers of the veteran whose memories have been stirred at the site of the great conflict .... Even in broad daylight, as one explores the line, a feeling unconsciously creeps over one that it is well to keep a weather-eye open toward the enemy's position, much akin to the state of mind of a skirmish-line feeling for an unseen foe – to be shaken off, of course, with a laugh ....

> Unknown Veteran of the Battle of Gettysburg, from "The Old Camp Ground," Grand Army Review, 1888.

My initial attention to the subject of the Confederate dead at Gettysburg began while completing research for a book on the wounded and the field hospitals of that renown battle. The tragedy of thousands of wounded men, many dying, left in these lonely, out-of-the-way places, so far from home was so overwhelmingly pathetic that their story begged to be told. Perhaps the most melancholy aspect of the whole unfortunate situation was the many Confederates who, although responsible for the war and most recently the invasion of the North, were now paying for their sins and those of their leaders in a most frightful way. And the ultimate penalty for their error was to die a painful, filthy, desolate death; then to be buried in an unmarked grave on a secluded creek bank, or under the foul mud at the rear of a Pennsylvanian's bank barn, or under the drooping branches of a solitary tree standing in a meadow, the "hallowed" site soon obliterated by the heedless blade of an enemy's plow.

There has always been a certain interest in the Southern dead at Gettysburg. A primary reason may be the fact that the disposition of the Union dead is well known and their story is often and eloquently told. The mere circumstance that many of the Northern soldiers who were killed were almost immediately transferred to a beautiful and distinctive burial ground, their mortal remains consecrated by President Lincoln and others, leaves little doubt in the minds of visitors to Gettysburg as to the whereabouts or sanctity of these men. Therefore, naturally, many who travel to the battlefield park are curious as to what exactly happened to the Southerners who fell in the battle. And of course, persons from below the Mason-Dixon line, especially if they are aware of an ancestor in the Army of Northern Virginia, may be anxious to know the other side of the story.

11

Now, anyone interested in this topic will have the opportunity of finding answers to many questions. This book covers not only a summary of events leading from the deaths of the rebel soldiers and the grisly scenes of the field, but also the early burials, and the final exhumation and transfer of these dead to the South. In subsequent parts are listed some names of the dead, the locations of the burial sites themselves, and finally, personal accounts of the last moments of fifty Confederate soldiers who were killed or mortally wounded between July 1 and 3, 1863. Also included are several appendices which give additional information on parallel topics.

It is my intention here to document a neglected theme within the Battle of Gettysburg's great storehouse of material. In addition, my wish to you, the reader, is that with this book you may find a greater understanding of a sensitive and important subject in American military history, a subject which intensely affected so many people for the rest of their lives.

Gregory A. Coco
January 10, 1990

Photograph Credits

The photographs in this book were, with two exceptions, taken by the author, who must bear the full blame for their worth. The purpose for the contemporary "burial site" photos is to document the locations in 1990, in order that future generations may see how, with so little restrictions on development in Adams County, these valuable historic areas stand the test of time. These scenes might also assist the present day visitor in finding the old grave locations, in the same manner as he or she would seek out a field hospital on a local farm or some other obscure portion of the battlefield.

The few photographs of the Confederate soldiers which have been included were borrowed from various books now in print, where they in turn were often second or third generation copies themselves. Therefore no special source identification seemed necessary.

The Southern soldier on the back of the dust jacket is a circa 1861 ambrotype in the author's collection kindly photographed by William A. Frassanito.

On the front cover is the famous Timothy O'Sullivan view taken on July 5, 1863. This print, and others in the collection of the U.S. Army Military History Institute, were copied by the publisher, Dean S. Thomas. Kathy Harrison analyzed this scene and writes:

> This ... photograph apparently shows the temporary burial, the hastily dug and sometimes unfinished graves, of Confederate dead at the Rose barn. The barn itself would be to the left, out of the photograph, and the grave is located just north of the barn ramp area. The whitewashed board fence in the background of the photograph is that which enclosed the lane leading from the Emmitsburg Road to the buildings and just beyond the house to the springhouse. The spaced trees in the background are probably orchard trees of the farm which were south of the lane. The tree tops just visible on the horizon line are the tops of the oaks in Biesecker Woods, on the west side of the Emmitsburg Road. An examination of the original photograph shows the groove marks in the headboards of the dead Confederates which apparently was the Rose flooring which was included in the claims file, taken from the barn . . . .

Of all of the visitors to the George Rose farm during the days, weeks, and months after the battle, only two are known to have recorded names found on the few headboards or grave markers in that area where so many unknown bodies lay. The two men were John B. Linn and Edward A. Bird,

13

and the names they wrote down are noted in Part I. It is very possible that one or more of the soldiers lying in the uncovered grave in this photograph were identified by Bird or Linn, and someday enough of the lettering on the headboards may be enhanced to decipher a name of one of these unfortunate men.

A note of thanks must also include Karen Lee Finley and Robert H. Prosperi who graciously assisted my many requests for photographic information during numerous research visits to the Gettysburg National Military Park Library.

List of Maps

PART I

A Charnel House of Death

When the splendor, the pomp and the circumstance of battle's magnificently stern array have gone, then the horrible and the ghastly only remain and remain in their most terrible forms.

> J. Howard Wert
> Gettysburg civilian

And what is the reward of those brave men for their weeks of weary marching, and days and nights of fearful fights? - Two paces of the vilest earth!

> Henry C. Morhous
> 123rd New York Infantry

The rebel dead, almost without exception, are buried promiscuously in single graves or trenches, where they lie unwept and unhonored.

> L.L.H., an unidentified visitor[1]
> to Gettysburg in early July, 1863.

Initial Appearance of the Field

For the families of soldiers who fought in the Battle of Gettysburg, the weeks, months, and even years of waiting for news of a precious son, father, husband, or brother, seemed to go on forever. And for many, especially Southerners whose young men were last seen at innocent sounding (but deadly) places like the Peach Orchard and the Wheatfield, Round Top or Culp's Hill, the waiting *would* last forever.

Indeed, the human harvest had been bountiful in Adams County, Pennsylvania in 1863. Like the farmers' harvest they replaced, the dead were everywhere. And as a volunteer nurse noted, each grave had its own history. Various estimates throughout the ensuing decades placed the number of Confederate bodies left on and around the battlefield, an area of about thirty-five square miles, somewhere between an estimated high of 4,500 to a low figure of 2,592.[2] [3]

Officially, Union General George G. Meade gave the numeration of

17

Confederate burials as 2,954 officers and men.* However, this summation did not include the large portion buried by the Eleventh and Twelfth Corps, nor the unknown number the Confederates buried themselves. One can not be sure that this total also included Southerners interred at the hospitals, along the retreat route, or others scattered indiscriminately throughout other parts of the campaign area, since the question asked Meade was only "How many Confederate dead were buried after the *battle* of Gettysburg?"

It is notable that on July 5 Meade, who was preparing to pursue General Robert E. Lee's retreating army, wrote to headquarters in Washington, "I cannot delay to pick up the debris of the battle-field . . . . My wounded, with those of the enemy in our hands, will be left at Gettysburg. After burying our own, I am compelled to employ citizens to bury the enemy's dead."[4]

In any event, bodies were plentiful enough; and grisly scenes abounded. And as one soldier recalled after viewing the area in front of the left center of the Union line, "I found my head reeling, the tears flowing and my stomach sick at the sight. For months the spectre haunted my dreams, and even after forty seven years it comes back as the most horrible vision I have ever conceived."[5]

During the summer of 1863, visitors to the fields of Gettysburg shared the same revulsion. Soldiers and civilians alike found much to satisfy each and every morbid curiosity as they treaded across the bloody ground both during the combat and in the days and even hours after the clash of hostilities had stilled.

On July 2 Henry Berkely, a Confederate artilleryman passing over an area northwest of the town, saw

> a sight which was perfectly sickening and heart-rending in the extreme. There were, within a few feet of us, by actual count, 79 North Carolinians laying dead in a straight line. I stood on their right and looked down their line. It was perfectly dressed. Three had fallen to the front, the rest had fallen backwards; yet the feet of all these dead men were in a perfectly straight line. The regiment belonged to Iverson's brigade . . . .[6]

Two days later and about a half mile southwestward, Lieutenant Robert Stiles recoiled from the rotting dead of July 1 which remained unburied along the Chambersburg Pike.

> The sights and smells that assailed us were simply indescribable - corpses swollen to twice their original size, some of them actually burst

---

*It should be mentioned that at least one *woman's* corpse was discovered on the field. It is highly likely that a number of women were in the ranks of both the Army of Northern Virginia and the Army of the Potomac. A few more may have been killed. We know of at least one other female rebel who was wounded and captured.

asunder with the pressure of foul gases and vapors. I recall one feature never before noted, the shocking distention and protension of the eyeballs of dead men and dead horses. Several human or unhuman corpses sat upright against a fence, with arms extended in the air and faces hideous with something very like a fixed leer, as if taking a fiendish pleasure in showing us what we essentially were and might at any moment become. The odors were nauseating, and so deadly that in a short time we all sickened and were lying with our mouths close to the ground, most of us vomiting profusely.[7]

Visiting this same place one day after Lieutenant Stiles, a Union colonel found the bodies literally bursting out of their clothes, with perfectly black faces. He saw burial details at work, ineffectually interring these unfortunates, putting twenty or more in trenches side by side, but covered with only a foot or two of earth. This officer exaggerated somewhat when he reported that he heard of 5,000 rebels having been buried so far.[8]

Toward the southern extremity of the battlefield was the infamous "slaughter pen," near to and including the vail between Little Round Top and Big Round Top. It presented a hideous sight to all who chose to venture into this gloomy and forlorn spot. A Massachusetts volunteer cautiously entered this area at midnight on July 3. The warm and muggy night was barely pierced by the "dim and sickly" light of the moon. A thin fog lay near the ground. The cedar and scrub oaks and scattered boulders barred the way as he and his companion saw,

Visitors often described the many Confederate corpses scattered throughout the "slaughter pen", an area near and east of the Devil's Den.

19

bodies . . . in every conceivable position, some with hand uplifted and teeth clenched, others with a smile of peace . . . . The majority had a settled, determined expression, as though they had a revengeful feeling in their hearts. Some were in the act of tearing cartridges, others just loading or reaching for the rammer . . . . We came suddenly upon a young boy caught and stiffened in the forked branches of a small cedar, looking like a statue of marble, with its upturned face to the sky. His cap had dropped off, and his whole appearance was so natural, that it seemed impossible that he was not alive. It startled me so that for a few moments all walked along in silence.[9]

Many others were "startled" by such scenes. A Connecticut soldier recalled a comrade on a burial party shouting, "Lookout! There's a Johnny aiming at you!" The Johnny was there alright, but long dead, holding his musket in position across a large stone and his face down on the breech. He had been struck in the forehead in the act of firing, and was instantly killed.[10]

Sergeant W.S. White, 2nd U.S. Sharpshooters, may have viewed this same or a similar corpse shortly before he wrote this in his diary on July 5:

At another place we saw a rebel's body standing up almost straight beside a big rock. His rifle lay over the top of the stone and his arms were extended on top of the rock. From appearance, I should think he was about to fire when he was hit and instantly killed, falling forward on to the stone and as his body swelled, it straightened up so as to be in a standing position.

White also inspected Devil's Den where he found a rebel's body stuck in "the cleft of the big rock and was so bound in between the stones that it was impossible to get it out."[11]

Other bodies were seen there posed in very natural positions. One, a Confederate, with his back against a tree had his arms lying calmly across his breast, his musket leaning against the tree trunk. Another sat with his arms folded about his musket, his head drooped down as if he was a sentinel who had sat down to rest and had fallen asleep. One other Southerner, bending over a companion in the act of bandaging a wounded limb, had been instantly shot dead, his body falling upon his friend as both died together.[12]

Nearby, and also near Devil's Den, a Gettysburg civilian, Dan Skelly, walked over the field on July 6 and saw "twenty-six Confederate officers, ranking from a colonel to lieutenants, laid side by side in a row for burial. At the head of each was a board giving their names, ranks and commands to which they belonged. A short distance away was another group of thirteen arranged in the same way."[13]

Another local citizen, T. Duncan Carson, visiting a shadowy and eerie part of his uncle's farm just below Big Round Top, said that "eighteen hundred of the [rebel] dead were buried in a single trench. They were

One of the "horrors of the battlefield" so often recalled by early visitors to Gettysburg.

covered very shallow, and at night you could see phosphorescent light coming out of the earth where they were buried."

Carson was quick to point out too that there were few if any buzzards on the field during this early period after the battle. He flatly stated that all the birds had been frightened away by the smell of powder and noise of battle. Many other witnesses likewise attested to this observation.[14]

Not far away, in the "wheatfield" of George Rose's farm, Union soldiers were burying both Northerners and Southerners killed in that sector. A spectator here, James Houghton of the 4th Michigan, said that most were carried to a wooded area west of that wheatfield where the Federals there were carefully interred with blankets under their heads, etc. In some cases he stated, comrades washed out the bloody garments of their deceased friends in a brook which ran close by, dried them nearby and then dressed the bodies for burial. Houghton recalled that, "On the bank near the [rebel burial] trench Lye[s] a large Rebel Sargent [.] One of our miney balls had passed through His Head so quick that it dislocated all the Confederacy there was in it and it was gradually oozing out onto the ground for the flies to Diagnosis. It was said that He was the man that Stabed colonel Jeffords . . . . "[15]

From all sources it appears that the area of the field most visited by soldiers and civilians after the battle was the Culp's Hill section of the Union's three-mile defensive line which was named after the old patriarch, Henry Culp. General Richard Ewell's men of the Army of Northern Virginia's Second Corps presented a sombre vision as they lay in death among the rocks and trees on the slopes leading up to the famous hill.

Near the Federal breastworks bodies lay piled in profusion, one "near the angle of the works, defended by the 28th PA . . . . a gray-haired veteran of sixty, had died within a yard of the line." Further down, a Northerner

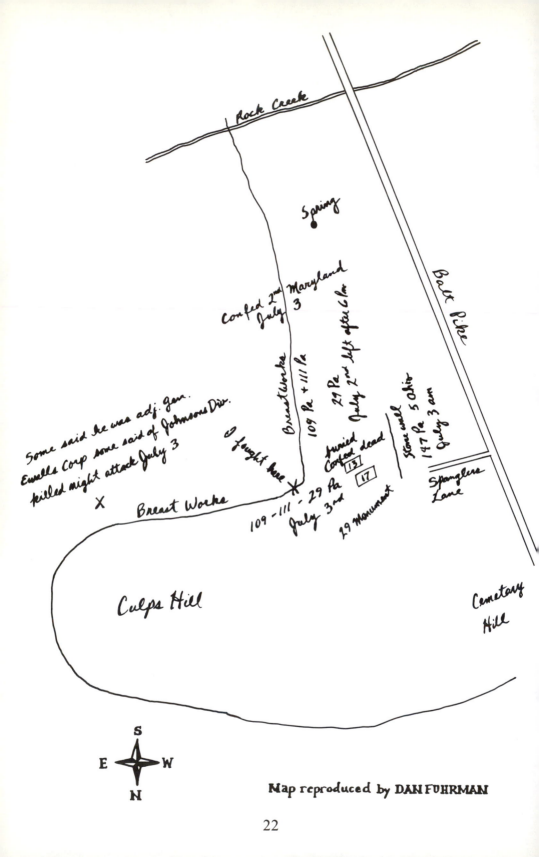

Rock Creek

Spring

Balt Pike

Confed 2nd Maryland
July 3

Breast Works
109 Pa + 111 Pa

29 Pa
buried July 2nd left after 6 pm

Stone wall
5 Ohio
147 Pa
July 3 am

Some said he was adj. gen.
Ewells Corp some said of Johnsons Div.
killed night attack July 3

X

I fought here

Breast Works

X

109 - 111 - 29 Pa
July 3rd

buried
Confed dead

13

17

29 Monument

Spanglers
Lane

Culps Hill

Cemetary
Hill

S
E ✦ W
N

Map reproduced by DAN FUHRMAN

22

The "angle" near Culp's Hill, in front of which so many Confederates fell, and their bodies were viewed by many curious sightseers.

Phila Oct 9-99
Col. John P. Nicholson

My dear sir
  Seeing an article in the Press of yesterday in reference to the finding of the dead bodies on Culp's Hill at Gettysburg & which were supposed to be Union dead. I write and send a crude diagram of my recollection of the place where we buried two separate lots of the Confederate dead on the morning of July 4. We also covered these bodies with our old blankets. . . . I do not know how the road runs where the bodies were found, but if it is anywhere near the spot I have designated the other lot of bodies should be nearby. There was one officer and 16 or 17 men in one lot and 13 men in the other.

Very truly yours,
David Monat
Co. G, 29th Pa. Vols.

23

The present day site of the two burial trenches which were dug by members of the 29th Pennsylvania and recorded by David Monat.

A post-war photograph of one of the many Confederate burial trenches which dotted the landscape around Culp's Hill.

found "a letter sticking out of the breastpocket of one of the confederate dead, a young man apparently about 24. Curiosity prompted me to read it. It was from his young wife away down in the state of Louisiana. She was hoping and longing [for his return home] . . . she says our little boy gets into my lap and says now Mama I will give you a kiss for Papa. But oh how I wish you could come home & kiss me for yourself."[16]

A Methodist minister riding along outside the five-foot-high log, stone and earthen breastworks on July 4 remembered Yankee soldiers still sitting behind the works, burying the dead, playing cards, or eating their suppers. The recent heavy rain had moistened the ground. He noticed a slight fog rising toward evening as he

> came to where a curve of the hill made an angle and [here I] saw one of the saddest sights to behold in life. About twenty or thirty dead men were lying in all positions on the ground. Some of them in groups huddled together. One especially attracted my attention. It was a boy apparently about twenty years of age. He lay with his head thrown back and his shirt pulled open in front. He had a beautiful face, jet black hair and skin as white as marble. The rain had washed the blood from his body and immediately above his heart was one small dark spot where the bullet entered that put out his life. I could not help thinking of the anxiety of some southern mother . . . .[17]

J. Howard Wert, a teenager who lived three miles southeast of Gettysburg on the Baltimore Pike, spent many days tramping over the recent field of strife. On July 4 at Culp's Hill, Wert saw piles of "dead as they were no where else, [anywhere] on the Gettysburg battle-field, on the same limited area." Young Wert, in the company of a furloughed army officer, stated that

As a young man, J. Howard Wert witnessed many distressing scenes around Gettysburg, including hundreds of unburied corpses.

25

even old soldiers, "stood aghast at the terrible picture of death there presented." He saw rebel bodies three deep in some places near the works, and an "area of four acres was so thickly covered it was scarcely possible to walk anywhere without treading on them."[18]

Westward from Culp's Hill at the "angle" where Alexander Webb's and other brigades had met the combination of the advance of Generals Trimble, Pettigrew, and Pickett on July 3, the land was much clearer and the beautiful view spread out for miles toward the low mountains to the west. Here, as one veteran recorded in his diary on July 5,

> was where the rebels charged up to the muzzles of the Union guns that were double shotted with canister and where several hundred of their dead bodies were laying almost in piles, and most of them terribly mutilated. It was a gruesome sight and a sight not to be forgotten.[19]

On Saturday, July 4, a young staff officer, Frank Haskell, estimated that the Second Corps buried hundreds of Southerners in their front, some having been killed on July 2, the rest in Longstreet's charge of the following afternoon.[20]

Daniel Skelly, mentioned earlier, said on July 6 that out toward the Emmitsburg Road, "there were still some dead Confederates who had not been buried. They were lying on their backs, their faces toward the heavens, and burned as black as coal from exposure to the hot sun." One officer, however, had evidently been interred there earlier. His grave is mentioned in at least four other accounts. Skelly noted, "It was close to the southern end of the [Nicholas] Codori barn .... It was the grave of a Confederate colonel." The wooden headboard had a Masonic emblem carved onto it. He was Joseph Wasden, 22nd Georgia Infantry, who had been killed on July 2.[21]

Another eyewitness of the terrible scenes at the "angle" was George Benedict, 12th Vermont Infantry, who, on July 4, beheld this sight:

> In the open ground in front of our lines on the centre and left, multitudes of the dead of both armies still lay unburied, though strong burial parties had been at work for twenty-four hours. They had died from almost every conceivable form of mutilation and shot-wound. Most of them lay on their backs with clothes commonly thrown open in front, perhaps by the man himself in his dying agony, or by some human jackal searching for money on the corpse, and breast and stomach often exposed. The faces, as a general rule, had turned black - not a purplish discoloration, such as I had imagined in reading of the 'blackened corpses' so often mentioned in descriptions of battle-grounds, but a deep bluish black, giving to corpse with black hair the appearance of a negro, and to one with light or red hair and whiskers a strange and revolting aspect. In the woods on our right, where the long musketry fight of Friday forenoon raged, I found the rebel dead (our own having been mostly buried) literally covering the ground. In a circle of fifty feet

radius as near as I could estimate, I counted forty-seven dead rebels. The number of the enemy's dead in two acres of that oak grove, was estimated at 2,000 and I cannot say that I think it exaggerated.[22]

This "color" of the bodies often attracted the attention of the curious. One soldier of the 141st Pennsylvania noted this peculiar aspect:

> I walked over a part of the battlefield and watched the burial parties at their work. One thing peculiar struck me, and that was the difference in appearance of the dead soldiers of the two armies. The rebel dead retained nearly their natural appearance, while our dead had almost invariably turned a very dark purple in the face. Why it was so I could not even guess.[23]

The town too had its share of rebel corpses. Albertus McCreary, a youngster living in the village, remembered that many sharpshooters had been active in buildings facing the Union lines. Many had been killed in these deadly duels or had died of unattended wounds. He said,

> Dead soldiers were everywhere. Near a small house lay the bodies of two Confederate soldiers, and on looking into the house I saw two others, one on a bed and the other on the floor. I went in to see if the one on the bed might not be alive. He was dead. He was a young man, and on his breast was a medal of some order. I was tempted to take it off, but I did not because I thought it might lead to his identification.[24]

The Early Burials and How They Were Accomplished

As we have just seen, the immediate appearance of the battlefield was anything but a pleasant sight. During the battle and the first days thereafter, corpses were evident on many parts of the contested ground. In fact, you could find just about anything in the way of sight or souvenir during those times. There was

> paper, envelopes, bits of letters, shreds of clothing, pieces of photo-graphs, muskets, bayonets, ramrods, knapsacks, haversacks, caps, old shoes and blankets, and many other articles were scattered everywhere. The trees were riddled with balls. We saw an iron ramrod so fastened in a tree that we could not pull it out . . . . Long trenches, heaped over with fresh earth, told where tens, twenties and fifties of rebels were interred. They boasted that in coming into [Pennsylvania] they had got back into the Union - many who thus boasted occupied those trenches. Their boasting had met a fearful verification.[25]

Although burial of the bodies had begun almost as soon as the battle started, the sad fact is that most were left until July 4 when the real work of interment began. For instance, on July 2 one soldier remarked: "The dead and dying covered the ground . . . . A few of the dead were buried, but chiefly preparations were being made for the morrow."[26]

Interestingly enough, by July 4 or 5 ground that had been held by the Confederate army for three days still contained a great number of dead, even many of their own. Details of rebel prisoners and Union soldiers were set to work on the gruesome task. Later they were joined by some civilians as Captain W. Willard Smith, with a squad from the provost marshal's detachment, began arresting citizens for looting the government property which littered the field. Those so detained usually spent from twenty-four to seventy-two hours with the burial parties, interring dead men and horses or digging sinks (latrines) at the field hospitals. In fact, on one particular day a visitor to the battlefield, a prominent judge from Philadelphia, was ordered to this hard labor for attempting to take a musket home after his visit.[27 28]

These men assigned to burial duties soon learned how their task could be made easier. One civilian reported:

> I went over to Culp's Hill Sunday [July 5]. They were burying the dead there in long narrow ditches about two feet deep. They would lay in a man at the end of the trench and put in the next man with the upper half of his body on the first man's legs and so on. They got them in as thick as they could and only covered them enough to prevent their breeding disease. All the pockets of the dead were turned out. Probably that was done by the soldiers who did the burying. They thought they might find a ring, or money, or something else of value.[29]

It is obvious by now that very little was done to identify the remains of the Confederates killed at Gettysburg. Confusion resulted, and erroneous information was widely spread concerning the whereabouts of missing sons, husbands or fathers. Leading officers of both armies, including a few generals, were incorrectly reported as being killed or wounded. Imagine then the uncertainty regarding the rank and file, especially in the Southern army. Newspapers of the time were filled with advertisements soliciting information concerning loved ones last seen somewhere in the ranks at Gettysburg. Many of these mysteries were never unraveled.

Even when the Confederates buried their own comrades, little time was given to mourning, precision, or identification. A South Carolina officer recalled:

> A detail from each company is formed into a squad, and armed with spades or shovels they search the field for the dead. When found a shallow pit is dug, just deep enough to cover the body, the blanket is taken from around the person, his body being wrapped therein, laid in the pit, and sufficient dirt thrown upon it to protect it from the vultures. There is no systematic work, time being too precious . . . . Sometimes friendly hands cut the name and the company of the deceased upon the flap of a cartridge box, nail it to a piece of board and place it at the head, but this was soon knocked down, and at the end of a short time all traces of the dead are obliterated.[30]

Unfortunately, identification tags were not in common use within Northern or Southern ranks, but some officers undoubtedly made attempts to properly identify their men killed in battle. Captain William C. Oates did just that. He reported that to avoid having his men buried by unfamiliar details and graves marked "unknown," he "procured and placed on their caps, 'Co. G, Fifteenth Alabama.' "[31]

Civilian Andrew Cross remarked that in some cases where time permitted, graves often *were* prepared with much more care and thoughtfulness. He wrote:

> . . . it is gratifying to see the respect shown, when opportunity is had, in the burying of individuals in spots, under trees, by a rock, near a stream, places where they can be found, with the inscription on a board, or cut in a tree or on a rock. Under a pear tree, near a house, a short distance north of the 11th Corps hospital, on the east side of the Taneytown road, [is] buried . . . Lieutenant E. G. Grannis of Macon, Ga . . . . In a field between Rock Creek and the turnpike . . . below the rocks, in the lower part of a meadow on the other side . . . is Marshall Prue, Company F, 5th Texas. A piece of rail, in each case, is driven in at the head of the grave, and the name written with a lead pencil.[32]

After some experience, many gravediggers began to use a common system, whereby half of the burial party collected the bodies into rows, and the other half dug the shallow holes. The first grave would be opened, a corpse placed in it and dirt from the next grave would cover the first body, and so on. This allowed the men to handle the dirt only once.

At Culp's Hill, Lieutenant Haskell wrote that,

> All along through these bullet-stormed woods were interspersed little patches of fresh earth, raised a foot or so above the surrounding ground. Some were very near the front of the works; and nearby, upon a tree whose bark had been smoothed by an ax, written in red chalk would be the words, not in fine handwriting, '75 Rebels buried here.' ☛ '54 Rebs. there.' And so on.[33]

J. Howard Wert said of the same place:

> The dead here were more carefully interred than on almost any other portion of the field. Deep, wide trenches were made in which the corpses were placed side by side and well covered. On an adjacent oak the burial parties would hew off the bark from one side and place in lead pencil the number buried in the trench; thus: '73 rebs buried to the right': '45 rebs, in this trench,' etc. There were seventeen of these trenches on a space not exceeding five or six acres, in which the numbers varied from a dozen to 70 or 80.[34]

The young civilian McCreary recalled that the "stench from the battle-field after the fight was so bad that everyone went about with a bottle of pennyroyal or peppermint oil. The burial of the dead commenced at once, and many were buried along the line where they fought and fell, and, in many cases, so near the surface that their clothing came through the earth."[35]

As the days passed the *battlefield* dead had been interred for the most part. By now, of course, the armies were far away leaving the remaining corpses to be handled by small squads of the provost marshal's office, local civilians, or a few remaining rebel prisoners. In fact, at least one local citizen, Samuel Herbst, was contracted by Assistant Quartermaster Captain W. G. Rankin to finish this work. Mr. Herbst, who evidently was already accomplished in this method of earning a living, must have commenced it permanently in 1863. At any rate his name appeared later in the 1880 records of the Gettysburg borough council when "the lot east of the jail was cleared of its 228 silent tenants by Samuel Herbst, and a force of exhumers; some of the remains being moved to the graveyard where the Reformed Church stands, and some to the old cemetery."[36]

Meanwhile, new graveyards were being established within an eight mile radius of Gettysburg as wounded Confederate prisoners continued to die in some of the sixty field hospitals scattered on all sides and beyond the town limits. The medical director of these many hospitals, Surgeon Henry Janes, reported in late July that there were still 5,456 rebels in twenty-four of these camps.

Some of these hospitals were quite large and had rather extensive burial sites. For instance, the J. Edward Plank farm just west of Gettysburg, a hospital of Hood's Division, had recorded on it over one hundred *identified* Southern graves. Francis Bream's tavern and farm on the Fairfield Road showed over sixty identified burials, and a field hospital at the old Jacob Hankey farm on the Mummasburg Road listed more than fifty. Even Union hospitals held their share. A startling example is the Jacob Schwartz farm along White Run and Rock Creek which boasted nearly two hundred graves of Confederates unsuccessfully treated there. By far, the largest hospital cemetery was situated on a ridge south of the York Pike in rear of the large U.S. General Hospital at Gettysburg named Camp Letterman. By December 1, 1863, this graveyard supposedly held over 1,200 burials, two-thirds of which were Southerners.[37]

In addition, Confederates were being buried in outlying sections of Adams County, on Lee's retreat route, in nearby towns, and elsewhere. For instance, Lieutenant Colonel Benjamin F. Carter, 4th Texas, a native of Tennessee, died in an improvised hospital in Chambersburg, Pennsylvania, and was buried in the Methodist Cemetery. Another, Colonel Isaac E. Avery, 6th North Carolina Infantry, died on the retreat and was buried in an oak coffin under a pine tree in a small cemetery overlooking the Potomac River at Williamsport, Maryland. His body was later recovered and properly interred in Hagerstown, Maryland.

Enlisted men fared worse, of course; many like the two Southern soldiers killed while on a foraging expedition in late June near Fort Loudon,

Colonel Benjamin Carter. Wounded in the great battle, he was eventually trans-ported as far as Chambersburg where he died. (R.K. Krick)

Another casualty of the battle, Colonel Isaac Avery was initially buried in a lonely grave near the Potomac River. (R.W. Iobst)

Pennsylvania, and are still buried near there. Similarly, two rebels were killed on June 29, in a skirmish with Union cavalry near the Baltimore Turnpike in the lower part of Westminster, Maryland, and were buried in the Union Church Yard. These men, St. Pierre Gibson and William M. Murray, would linger a long time in Yankee soil.[38]

Many such incidents were recalled such as this sad sight described by Surgeon D. G. Brinton on July 17, 1863, in Maryland. "Just before entering Funkstown we passed the scene of a cavalry fight that had occurred the day but one before. The dead were not yet all buried & we passed the nauseating spectacle of a rebel dragoon lying by the roadside, dead, half clothed, & bloated by two July days."[39]

The deaths and the burials seemed to be a never-ending process. In out-of-the-way places, far removed from the late battleground, someone would often stumble across a single, missed corpse.

One farmer recollected just such an event:

> A neighbor of ours . . . came to get some flour on Tuesday, and he said, 'Over here in the woods I found a dead man.'
>
> So father and I took a mattock and a shovel and went along with [him] to the spot where he had come across the body. There it was, all bloated up, seated leaning against a tree. We had to make a grave a rod or so away on account of the tree roots. It was impossible to handle the man to get him there, he was so decayed, and we hitched his belt to his legs and dragged him along, and no sooner did we start with him than his scalp slipped right off. We just turned him in on his side and covered him with earth.[40]

Later Visitors and the Results of Inadequate Burials

The often hasty, haphazard, and incomplete burials of both Union and Confederate casualties resulted in many unforgettable scenes for the later arrivals who came to view the field, visit the hospitals, or search for a missing relative. People who made their excursions to Gettysburg and its environs from several weeks to several months after that conflict were destined to witness numerous sad and macabre sights.

On or about July 21, one visitor reminisced:

> On the north side of Big Round Top and near the summit I saw the whitened bones of a Johnny who had killed or wounded 17 of our men during the night [of July 2]. He rolled a rock as big as a bushel basket ahead of him, while he crawled behind it. He could see our men toward the sky . . . . [After he was finally killed], they could not dig a grave there. They cut brush and laid it across him, head down hill . . . His head had rolled down hill some 10 feet; his shoes with the bones of his feet had fallen sidewise and lay there.[41]

Near Devil's Den a Christian Commission delegate noted:

When burying the many that were slain here, it was difficult to get earth to bury them, and in a few places they had to be covered over with stone. In the latter part of August...when passing over this ground in company with Rev. Dr. George Junkin, [General Thomas J. "Stonewall" Jackson's father-in-law] we found some of these men still unburied. It is generally supposed that these were all Rebels; but in several cases we found the bodies wrapped in the overcoat of our men.[42]

Contiguous to the now-famous copse of trees at the "angle" a young nurse, Jane Moore, wrote on July 26 of how she and a companion could,

. . . walk along the low stone wall or breastwork . . . passed the hillock of graves - the little forest of headboards scattered everywhere . . . . Oh how they must have struggled along that wall . . . ; beyond it two immense trenches filled with rebel dead, and surrounded with grey caps, attest the loss to them. The earth is scarcely thrown over them, and the skulls with ghastly grinning teeth appear, now that the few spadefuls of earth are washed away. In these trenches one may plainly see the rise and swell of human bodies; and oh how awful to feel that these are brethren - deluded and erring, yet brethren. Surely, no punishment can be too great for those whose mad ambition has filled these graves![43]

And in late October, 1863, conditions on this part of the field had deteriorated even further. A Pennsylvania militia soldier wrote:

At this point any part of the human frame can be picked. [Here] . . . the Rebel prisoners were made to bury their dead. They dug long trenches about ten inches deep, then would lay from fifty to one hundred in each trench, then throw clay along the middle of the rows of men leaving the head and feet entirely exposed. When I was last there the fields had the appearance of a vast bone yard . . . the bodies became so decomposed that the heads would drop off the men - would drop from the slightest touch. Since then the heads have been kicked like footballs over the field. The stench here is still intolerable . . . blankets . . . are clotted with blood; many of the hats and caps are besmeared with brains.

There is a good possibility that one of the lamentable skeletons so mentioned was that of Confederate General Richard B. Garnett who was killed in Longstreet's assault on Friday, July 3, but whose remains were never identified nor located.

Further south at Devil's Den or Houck's Ridge, the same militiaman said that,

I almost strangled from the effects of the smell caused partly by the decomposed bodies. The crevices [are] from ten to fifteen feet deep . . . . Some skeletons of late have been hooked up with iron hooks attached to long poles. You will remember the Rebels buried their own dead here. Scarcely any graves were dug here. They dragged them to where they could throw them into some crevices and tumbled them in and threw a

33

General Richard Garnett, whose body was never seen again after being interred by Union soldiers.

John Rose must have become hardened to the brutal scenes which surrounded his brother's farm.

few stones on them and thus left them. The visitor is shocked at every step while passing over the vast charnel house. As soon as the bodies began to decay the stones began falling down among the skeletons thus exposing all that each grave contains . . . . Here all the arms and legs that were shot off were not gathered and buried, but are lying about the rocks. I saw in a circle of one rod, four legs lying with shoes and stockings on. Whole hands lay withering in the sun.[44]

Several miles north of the den, in late July, a sightseer at the Lutheran Theological Seminary, Reverend E. W. Hutter, "saw 56 in one trench, forty two, without a solitary name inscribed. The spot itself is designated by a board nailed against a tree, with the inscription that here lies so many rebels. Seven soldiers are found within arms reach of Dr. [Charles B.] Krauth's rear door."

Hutter also observed that Dr. Samuel S. Schmucker's garden, also on the Seminary grounds, contained a number of Confederate graves.[45]

An interesting account of an early visit to Gettysburg was kept in a diary by John B. Linn, a Union soldier on leave from his regiment. Near the Nicholas Codori farm on July 8, he saw Colonel Wasden's grave and nearby,

15 unburied Rebels. We walked up to look at them, they were swollen large as giants, black in the face, but seemed to me to have an individuality which would render recognition by their friends even then possible. They had shirts, yellow pants and a leather belt on. Pockets of their pants were turned out . . . We proceeded about 1/2 mile beyond to [the] farm of Mr. [George] Rose . . . Here to the North of his barn we counted 33 graves of the 12th South Carolina Volunteers. They were only slightly covered with earth and you could feel the body by pressing the earth with your foot. One man's left hand (John B. Robbins, Co. I, 8th South Carolina Volunteers), stuck out of the grave looking like an old parched well worn buck-skin glove.

Further on, Linn came across the graves of other South Carolinians. He spoke to Mr. Rose who said he had recently moved ten colonels, majors and other officers, who had previously been buried in his garden, to another spot east of his house. Rose had not re-interred them, but had merely left each officer's headboard beside the body. Rose next pointed to his wheatfield saying that there were still fifty rebels lying unburied there.[46]

A similar account to Linn's is that of Edward A. Bird, a Baltimore civilian who traversed the field in late August, 1863. Near Round Top he encountered,

. . . men not half buried. It may be a skull, an arm, a leg protruding from the ground, barely in many instances covered over. I have seen the body slightly covered, and the skull being outside the grave . . . . In passing over the field in front of the Round Tops, I came across the graves of 35

Confederates of the 15th South Carolina Regiment. There was a Lieut. Col. buried along with them but there was no headboard to his grave. Amongst the names I took . . . Lt. W. L. Daniel, . . . E.I. Miles, . . . T.S. Gadsden, . . . S.C. Miles . . . a few hundred yards . . . and in front of the house, a few yards from the spring house [was] Capt. I.M.D. Bond, Co. I, 53rd Georgia, [and] Sergt. Alfred Berth, Co. I, 50th Ga. I also noticed a headboard (but not grave) with T. Glading, Co. E, 15th Regt. S. Ca., Vol., July 3rd 63. In the woods . . . were more Confederates . . . . Way down in one corner of a field and near the base of the Round Top, was the grave of a Texas soldier . . . his old coat being alongside of his grave.[47]

Several months later in mid-October, 45-year-old Erie, Pennsylvania resident Isaac Moorhead paid a short visit to the old battlefield. He met the local hero, John Burns, walked to the grave of Mary Virginia Wade, the young civilian casualty of the battle, and then took a carriage ride over the field with a local guide, Mr. J.G. Frey. He, too, saw Lieutenant Colonel Wasden's grave, now surrounded by a neat fence, and then came to a field where he said sixteen hundred rebels were buried. Moorhead continued:

> Dismounting among the rocks, [near Little Round Top] we saw some bones of a rebel, with shreds of his butternut clothing . . . [At Devil's Den he looked upon a] rebel's grave . . . just at the mouth of the den, and his boots I saw lying just within the den, thrown there by Mr. Frey at the burial of the rebel . . . . [Later] in a secluded spot among the rocks, I found the bones of a rebel just as he had fallen. Picking up one of his shoes...the bones of his foot tumbled out . . . . From among his ribs I picked up a battered minie ball which doubtless caused his death.
>
> Moving aside a flat stone, Mr. Frey showed us the grinning face and skull of a rebel. Some of them in this rocky part of the field have very shallow graves.
>
> [The next day] We stopped at the house of Peter Rogers [on the Emmitsburg Road] . . . . A rebel sharpshooter was killed on top of his house, and tumbled down in front of the door. Another died of exhaustion on the steps. Many were found dead in the yard. In a field behind the house several were buried; the feet of one stuck up through the ground. His skull was bare . . . . Passing along we saw where four rebel colonels were buried in a row. I think from their position they were General [Lewis] Armistead's colonels.[48]

Early Identification and Removal

As can be expected, immediately after hostilities were concluded, families and friends of men thought to be killed or wounded at Gettysburg came to Adams County to search for their cherished warriors. Naturally, most were Northerners, but a few Southern families managed to get word to people in Gettysburg to inquire for help with their sacred quest. The situation only worsened with the end of the war, and in truth became almost an embarrassment to the victors of that battle.

As a matter of fact, in early 1864, a local newspaper called for "a place to be set apart for the burial of the Confederate dead who are now buried promiscuously over the battlefield . . . . Common humanity would dictate a removal to some spot . . . where Southern friends may, when the rebellion is crushed . . . make their pilgrimage here."[49]

Several years passed before the citizenry below the Mason and Dixon Line were able to provide for the removal of some of the Southern remains. In the meantime several local men made the effort to record the names of deceased soldiers who lay in individual gravesites scattered near Gettysburg and throughout the county. A farmer, J.G. Frey, was one of the first to take an interest in this task. He kept an accurate journal of the location of many of the Union-marked graves prior to their removal to the Soldiers' National Cemetery.

Another concerned civilian was Dr. J.W.C. O'Neal, a native of Fairfax County, Virginia, who had attended Pennsylvania College in Gettysburg, and had received his medical degree from the Maryland Medical School. O'Neal had practiced in Baltimore and Hanover, Pennsylvania, before permanently moving his office to Gettysburg in early 1863. Shortly after the

Dr. John O'Neal did more than any other person to honor and protect the thousands of deceased Southerners left at Gettysburg.

Sam Weaver; another who assisted in retaining the identity and location of many of the Confederate graves in Adams County. (Hanover Chamber of Commerce)

battle Dr. O'Neal began to keep a record of the names and burial places of many of the Confederates so recently killed. He worked together with Samuel Weaver, the Gettysburg resident who had assisted David Wills, agent for Governor Andrew Curtin of Pennsylvania, in removing the remains of many Union soldiers to the Soldiers' National Cemetery. Together, O'Neal and Weaver helped in the location and transfer to the South of a number of Confederate bodies, mostly officers of prominent or wealthy families who could afford such an expensive and time-consuming undertaking. Faithfully over a ten-year period, Weaver and O'Neal retained the identities of at least 1,200 individual Confederate soldiers who otherwise might have been lost to history. An example of the kind of communication they often received during the years from 1863 to 1870 is this letter from Mrs. A.T. Mercer, who had lost her 21-year-old- son, Captain Oliver F. Mercer, of the 20th North Carolina Infantry, killed in battle on July 1.[50]

> Our Wilmington papers bring the welcome intelligence to many bereaved Southern hearts that you have cared for the graves of many of our Confederate dead at Gettysburg, replaced headboards and *prepared a list of names.* May the Lord bless you is the prayer of many Southern hearts - Oh! we have lost so much. There are but few families that do not mourn the loss of one or more loved ones, and only a mother who has lost a son in that awful battle can and does appreciate fully such goodness as you have shown. I, too, lost a son at Gettysburg, a brave,

38

noble boy in the full bloom of youth, and my heart yearns to have his remains, if they can be found, brought home to rest in the soil of the land he loved so well. I need your assistance and I am confident you will aid me. No sorrow-stricken mother could ask and be refused by such a heart as yours.[51]

Obviously, from such sentiments, a high value was placed on the good works of these gentlemen.

Also, it is interesting to note that in the fall of 1863, a map had been prepared by a Philadelphia civil engineer named S.G. Elliott. Although far from completely accurate, it did present very likely the first and only surviving survey of many of the large burial sites of both Union and Confederate graves. Unfortunately, Elliott only listed the *identities* of about ten Confederates on his map. And in places where only forty or fifty rebels had actually been buried, he incorrectly listed *four hundred* or *five hundred* graves. In any event, the map has served a useful purpose through the years.[52]

The Final Solution

By the late 1860s a great interest and desire had sprung up in the South that all the remaining Confederate soldiers who had been killed outright or had died of wounds near Gettysburg should find a permanent resting place among their kindred. Appeals from several Ladies' Memorial Associations in the cities of Raleigh, Savannah, Charleston, and Richmond went to Dr. Rufus Benjamin Weaver of Philadelphia. Dr. Weaver, the son of Samuel

Dr. Rufus Weaver, reluctant and unpaid pawn in the movement to remove and reinter the Southern dead back to their homeland.

Hollywood Cemetery in Richmond, Virginia, where many of the Gettysburg dead lie today unknown and unmourned. (Mary H. Mitchell)

and Elizabeth Weaver of Gettysburg, had earlier assisted his father in the recording and the transference of Federal and Confederate bodies on and near the battlefield. After Samuel's death in 1871, Rufus Weaver gained possession of his father's extensive records; he also had wide knowledge of the location of individual and mass graves and had become intimate with the Adams County landowners. For these reasons the ladies' societies especially wanted Dr. Weaver to supervise the final and total removal of all Southern remains from Gettysburg. Although he was an extremely busy physician working as Demonstrator of Anatomy in the Hahnemann Medical College at Philadelphia, Weaver finally consented to help the societies as time could be spared from his professional commitments. His obituary read that:

> During the summers of 1871, '72 and '73 he superintended the work of opening graves, identifying the remains and sending them to that society representing the particular section of the South to which the dead belonged. During these three years he forwarded the remains of seventy-four to Charleston, S.C., one hundred and thirty-seven to Raleigh, N.C., one hundred and one to Savannah, Ga., and two thousand nine hundred and thirty-five to Richmond, Va.[53]

Dr. Weaver also removed seventy-three remains for various private individuals. The official total for his three years of work was 3,320 remains shipped to the South for which he was owed $9,536.00* by the societies. When possible, he included identifications of the soldiers as well as the various personal articles that were found interred with them. As can be contemplated, his problems were endless.

For instance, Weaver actually had to make several trips to the farm of David Blocher, just north of Gettysburg, to recover a gold dental plate which had been removed from the skull of Lieutenant Colonel David R.E. Winn, 4th Georgia Infantry. He eventually had to pay Oliver Blocher, the son, $5.00 for the plate before it could be reunited with Colonel Winn's skeleton.[54]

Ironically, as careful as Dr. O'Neal and Samuel and Rufus Weaver had been in preserving many individual Confederate identities, when the bones arrived at their final resting places in Southern private or public cemeteries, most were unfortunately simply piled into mass graves where they remain today. A prime example of this occurred at Hollywood Cemetery in Richmond. The very pride of the South which had worked so diligently to remove their sons from the "vile sod of the North," now indiscriminately and forever erased many of these fallen heroes from existence.

---

*This debt was never paid; even as late as 1887 Dr. Weaver was still trying to collect the $9,500 plus interest.

Conclusion

Present-day visitors to the battlefield park often ask the question, "What happened to the Confederates who were killed and buried here?" After hearing the answer, many will reply, "Are there any bodies remaining?" The response is a very definite yes.

Reasoning that a total of at least 4,500 to 5,000 Confederate soldiers were killed or died during the campaign, and only about 3,400 were disinterred to the South, then it is plausible that as many as 1,500 individual remains were never recovered. It is now known, for instance, due to the important research of John W. Busey and Roy Frampton, that at least ten Southerners were mistakenly buried in the Soldiers' National Cemetery which was so beautifully and eloquently dedicated by Edward Everett, Abraham Lincoln and other prominent Northern leaders. Also known is that over fifty rebel remains were discovered while erecting monuments and building avenues in the 1880s and 1890s on what is now the Gettysburg National Military Park. And a host of newspaper accounts demonstrate that from the 1870s through the 1940s bodies of both Confederate and Union soldiers were often excavated while work was being done on many parts of the battlefield.

Examples abound such as: "Another skeleton of a Confederate soldier was found on the old 'Tapeworm' railroad track last Friday. The skull had a bullet hole and a bullet. The bones were interred at another place nearby."[55]

In all likelihood, most of the undiscovered graves of these unfortunate men will remain at Gettysburg forever. Like their brothers on thousands of battlefields throughout recorded and unrecorded history, they have been dealt their unhappy potion of life. Whether they died in wars that were accepted by their fellow creatures (most who were non-combatants, of course) as just or unjust, avoidable or unavoidable, becomes a moot point for them. The fact is and will remain, then and now, that the combat soldier, especially the infantryman, is often sacrificed at the whim and pleasure of and for the sake of the selfish and self interest of an entire nation or a few individuals. Most of these lives were thrown away, and were cheapened by the very way in which they were slaughtered.

Hundreds and thousands of unburied soldiers described as "black and bloated, eyes open and glaring, and corruption running from their mouths" is not a very enticing prescription for glory.[56]

Yes, at Gettysburg there was valor and glorious deeds and pride and love of country and maybe even a good reason; but for the Confederate dead who gained nothing - it was simply waste.

Mathew Brady's July 1863, view of the Plum Run Valley where some Confederate remains may still rest.

PART II

Southern Names, Northern Graves

Alas! in how many Southern homes aching hearts waited through weary months for news of loved ones that never came until the void of suspense was replaced by the dread certainty that the absent one had helped to swell the unknown dead of the Wheatfield, the Peach Orchard, or the Devil's Den of a Northern land.[57]

> J. Howard Wert
> Adams County Citizen

The initial objective of this section of the book was to compile a complete list of the approximately 1,200 Southern soldiers whose names, regiments, and burial locations had survived somewhat intact between 1863 and 1873. Two things prevented this from being implemented. The first and most important was that although on the surface O'Neal's and Weaver's lists *appeared* to be accurate — names and regiments were plain to see, however, on close inspection, and upon researching this supposedly factual information, it was found in a great many cases to be not only incorrect, but often impossible to verify. This meant that of the 1,200, only a certain percentage would or could be honestly identified. The second reason for not using all 1,200 names was the issue of space and cost. The addition of this large number of soldiers, regiments, and burial sites would push the cost of this book far beyond that which the author and publisher determined would be fair to the buyer. Therefore, a sampling of approximately 100 names was chosen, using about ten from each Southern state. These examples should give a good grasp of where certain Confederates were buried, which, as you shall read, is both interesting and unfailingly pathetic — these lonely places where men lay for long periods in the cold, alien ground, so very far from home.[58]

ALABAMA

H.P. Caffey Co. H, 3rd Ala.	From Lowndes County. Died of wounds Sept. 13. Interred initially at the Schwartz farm, but on May 30, 1866, was reinterred in a grave in Lot 169, Sec. E, in Evergreen Cemetery.
James B. Colquitt Co. G, 6th Ala.	David Schriver's or Rodes' Div. Hospital north of house, corner of orchard.
Berry Crow Co. F, 6th Ala.	Section 7, Grave 33, at Camp Letterman General Hospital.
Capt. James T. Davis Co. D, 12th Ala.	J.S. Forney farm, Mummasburg Rd.
Burton L. Hardman Co. K, 13th Ala.	Maj. Samuel Lohr's, 4 miles out the Chambersburg Turnpike opposite his house in the meadow and under a pear tree.
Pvt. John H. Haynes Co. B, 8th Ala.	Francis Bream's farm in field near woods, along side of Adam Butt's woods near run.
Capt. William W. Leftwich Co. F, 4th Ala.	Died at Hood's Div. Hospital on J.E. Plank's farm on the bank of Willoughby's Run.
Sgt. J.R. McLean Co. A, 9th Ala.	Buried north of Adam Butt's, Anderson's Div. Hospital, was placed under cherry tree [toward] Mr. Bream's.
William O'Mearra Co. F, 5th Ala.	[Moses McClean] farm 3/4 mile northwest of Gettysburg south along the lane in cherry thicket.
Harvey Perryman Co. K, 14th Ala.	Twelfth Corps Hospital [George Bushman's] 3 1/2 miles southeast of Gettysburg.
J.N. Robertson Co. B, 4th Ala.	Yard B, Second Corps Hospital on Jacob Schwartz's farm about 4 miles southeast of Gettysburg.

ARKANSAS

Christopher C. Beeman Co. G, 3rd Ark.	Wounded July 2, died July 10 and buried under tree on the right of [Plank's] house.
Sgt. James W. Castleman Co. H, 3rd Ark.	North of [J.E. Plank's] house under walnut tree. From Hardin County, Kentucky, wounded thigh July 2; frame around grave; under tree to right of house, grave arranged by stones.
L.R. Noble Co. K, 3rd Ark.	Wounded thigh, July 2; died July 7, covered with stones; under tree to right of house at Plank's.
M. Reeves Co. K, 3rd Ark.	North side of Plank's house under a walnut tree. Wounded hip July 2; died July 18.
Stephen A. Wallace Co. B, 3rd Ark.	Section 4, Grave 35, Camp Letterman General Hospital burial ground.

FLORIDA

Sgt. Felix M. Bryant
Co. F, 8th Fla.

Pennsylvania College – north side – [of] building used as General Early's Div. Hospital

Sgt. William C. Butler
Co. F, 2nd Fla.

Section 1, Grave 37, Camp Letterman General Hospital burial ground.

Ellis Padgett
Co. E, 8th Fla.

Yard B, Second Corps Hospital, Mr. Schwartz's about 4 miles S.E. of Gettysburg.

S.J. Sanchez
Co. B, 2nd Fla.

Died July 17, Grave 16 back of barn on J. Schwartz's farm.

GEORGIA

Albert L. Allen
Co. A, 16th Ga.

Michael Fiscel farm [Fifth Corps Hospital] east of house across the creek, 5 miles down Baltimore Pike.

Cpl. William R. Butler
Co. H, 4th Ga.

Killed July 1 – buried opposite Negro church on Long Lane.

Frank Butts
Co. K, 61st Ga.

Killed July 1. Josiah Benner's farm in meadow along fence.

Maj. Thomas Camak
Cobb's Ga. Legion

Age 33. At John Cunningham's place, across creek from John Crawford's.

Sgt. Joseph R. Crutchfield
Co. D, 2nd Ga. Battalion

Wounded July 2; died July 27; Yard B, Row 2 between J. Schwartz and G. Bushman at Second Corps Hospital.

Thomas A. Elmore
Co. A, 7th Ga.

Wounded head and arm, July 2; died July 7. Buried on the J.E. Plank farm, Hood's Div. Hospital.

Capt. John C. Fraser
Pulaski Ga. Artillery

John S. Crawford's farm under tree on road from mansion to tenant house.

John R. Gibson
Co. G, 22nd Ga.

Widow J. Young's 4 miles down the Baltimore Turnpike. Died July 14.
Also shown as buried on Samual Durboraw farm near tavern. [The two farms were adjacent.]

William J. Hogans
Co. A, 48th Ga.

West of D. McMillan's in woods (close by Gen. Pickett's line).

Alexander A. McCrary
Co. E, 9th Ga.

Wounded chin and neck July 2; died July 5. Under locust tree towards Crawford's on J.E. Plank farm on the bank of Willoughby's Run.

Thomas N. Ray
Co. K, 22nd Ga.

At Pennsylvania College north side of building used as Gen. Early's Div. Hospital.

Robert R. Walker
Co. G, 8th Ga.

Buried on Wm. Douglas' farm under a large oak tree to the rear of the extreme Confederate right.

Colonel Samuel P. Lumpkin, 44th Georgia lost a leg amputated at Gettysburg, and died at Hagerstown, Maryland. (R.K. Krick)

LOUISIANA

John R. Barrett
La. Guard Artillery

Northwest corner of field on Joseph B. Leas farm 4 miles east of Gettysburg.

William Ford
Co. B, 7th La.

Age 24. Leg amputated, died Aug. 29. Row 4, Grave 35, Camp Letterman General Hospital burial ground.

George H. Jamison
Co. B, 8th La.

Killed July 1. Buried north or back of John Crawford's brick house toward Almshouse along fence.

Thomas McCarty
Co. I, 8th La.

From Baton Rouge. Buried at George Spangler's in Twelfth Corps Hospital graveyard.

James H. McElroy
Co. A, 1st La.

Killed July 2. Grave along Hunterstown Rd. on W.H. Monfort farm, 1st brick house from York Pike. Age 25.

Louis Thibaut
La. Guard Artillery

Killed July 1. Grave near state road at Elizabeth Weible's farm, back of barn.

Major Henry
L.N. Williams
9th La.

John Crist's farm under gum tree [Chambersburg Rd.].

MARYLAND

William S.J. Chandler
Co. A, 1st Md. Battalion

George Bushman's Twelfth Corps Hospital, north side of barn.

Cpl. Daniel Dougherty
Chesapeake Md. Artillery

From Baltimore. Along south side of Hanover Road on Daniel Lady's farm opposite the stone house.

48

James Nash
Co. C, 1st Md. Battalion
Pennsylvania College north side of building used as Gen. Early's Div. Hospital.

William L. Nichols
Co. C, 1st Md. Battalion
Died Aug. 13. Camp Letterman General Hospital, 1st Row, Grave 14.

Thaddeus Parker
Chesapeake Md. Artillery
At Christian Benner's farm back of Rock Creek under a large walnut tree.

John Sullivan
Co. E, 1st Md. Battalion
Died Aug. 1. David Stewart farm 2 miles from Fairfield.

MISSISSIPPI

Lt. Geo. W. Bradley
Co. A, 13th Miss.
John Trostle's in corner of field on bank of Rock Creek.

Adj. M.R. Campbell
48th Miss.
East of Emmanuel Pitzer's house in meadow.

B.G. Coleman
Co. A, 19th Miss.
At Adam Butt's farm, south of house near road toward F. Bream's.

Capt. Henry Davenport
Co. E, 42nd Miss.
Cemetery D at J. Schwartz's farm, the Second Corps Hospital site.

Daniel S. King
Co. A, 17th Miss.
At John S. Crawford's farm in garden.

James N. Lesley
Co. C, 2nd Miss.
20 years old. Died Oct. 5. Row 9, Grave 2, Camp Letterman General Hospital.

Cpl. R. Lewis McLaurin
Co. A, 18th Miss.
Near Felix's place, along road on the left side going to S. Pitzer's under a locust or walnut tree out in the field, (at bend of road on Marsh Creek).

Charles Moore
Co. F, 13th Miss.
Left leg amputated. Died July 7. Buried in orchard on Marsh Creek on J.S. Crawford farm.

Lt. W.R. Oursler
Co. F, 17th Miss.
On road near Negro blacksmith shop near Peach Orchard (Warfields).

NORTH CAROLINA

Adolphus L. Campbell
Co. C, 28th NC
Twelfth Corps Hospital at George Bushman's farm.

Cpl. W.H. Flowers
Co. C, 4th NC Cavalry
Died July 5 at Gatehouse above Monterey Springs. Killed in a skirmish on July 4 in Gen. Kilpatrick's charge on one of Lee's wagon trains.

Lt. James A. Griffith
Co. G, 14th NC
At the foot of John S. Forney's garden along Mummasburg Rd.

Lt. Frank M. Harney
Co. F, 14th NC
At David Shriver's farm on Mummasburg Pike.

John C. Huson
Co. F, 1st NC
In meadow at Martin Shealer's farm next to Mrs. Elizabeth Weible's.

J.D. Leaman Co. D, 52nd NC	Buried east of Dr. Samuel E. Hall's in woods near county road.
Cameron L. Lenhardt Co. I, 11th NC	Eleventh Corps Hospital burial ground.
Lewis Mock Co. G, 2nd NC Battalion	Age 22. At Jacob Plank's, Millerstown Rd. [Fairfield] left side above F. Bream's – buried back of barn.
Capt. Elijah G. Morrow Co. G, 28th NC	On a hill under a walnut tree between J. Schwartz and G. Bushman's – 2nd row.
Archibald Nixon Co. G, 52nd NC	40 years old. Jacob Schwartz cornfield, Yard D, 1st row, on Second Corps Hospital grounds.
Maj. Egbert A. Ross 11th NC	21 years old. South of F. Herr's farm along Chambersburg Rd., in woods.
Lt. Iowa Michigan Royster Co. G, 37th NC	Corner of woods on south side of Henry Beitler's tenant house.
Capt. William Wilson Co. B, 26th NC	Charles Polley's farm northwest of Gettysburg on Chambersburg Pike. Killed July 1 "while gallantly leading his men up the hill through McPherson's [Herbst] woods."

Captain William Wilson died with sword in hand charging the enemy on July 1.

SOUTH CAROLINA

John Bligh Co. D, 2nd SC	Northwest of George Rose's and north of Emmitsburg Rd. along fence near some trees.
Lt. Milton P. Buzhardt Co. B, 3rd SC	On Marsh Creek north of F. Bream's tavern near burial place.
William P. Casey Brooks SC Artillery	Age 19. John S. Crawford's farm, east of tenant house where Samuel Johns lives.

Capt. W.P. Cromer Co. D, 13th SC	Oak Ridge; among 14 other remains; chiefly of Johnson's Div.
Lt. James M. Daniel Co. E, 7th SC	Killed July 3. On road near Pitzer's Schoolhouse in the field near fence.
Christian V. Hammond Co. B, 1st SC Rifles	Near county road at handboard that stands between S. Pitzer's and J. Socks under wild cherry tree.
Lt. M.R. Hinson Co. H, 2nd SC	Died July 3. Back of F. Bream's Tavern lot.
Cpl. Andy Martin Brooks SC Artillery	At Samuel Johns tenant house east of barn.
Sgt. Henry M. Paysinger Co. C, 3rd SC	Camp Letterman General Hospital burial ground, Row 7, no. 12. Died Sept. 5. 23 years old.
Capt. Robert C. Pulliam Co. B, 2nd SC	In center of F. Bream's burying ground.
Sgt. David R. Ryan Co. E, 2nd SC	George Rose's stone barn under cherry tree.
Lt. Albert J. Traylor Co. C, 7th SC	About 10 miles NW of Gettysburg near Cashtown under a chestnut tree on Isaac Rife's farm.

TENNESSEE

Hartwell H. Bradshaw Co. G, 7th Tenn.	Burial yard B. on hill between J. Schwartz and G. Bushman farms.
Francis M. Frazor Co. E, 7th Tenn.	At Maj. Samuel Lohr's. 4 miles out on the Chambersburg Turnpike opposite his house in meadow, near and under a pear tree.
Capt. Asaph Hill Co. F, 7th Tenn.	Yard D, Second Corps Hospital at the Jacob Schwartz farm.
Lt. James M. Manley Co. G, 1st Tenn.	28 years old. Camp Letterman General Hospital burial ground York Rd., 3rd Row, grave 12. Died Aug. 6.

TEXAS

John W. Brown Co. L, 1st Tex.	24 years old. At J.E. Plank's, Hood's Div. Hospital under tree, right and front of house toward Millerstown Rd. and Gettysburg.
John C. Graham Co. F, 4th Tex.	Died Aug. 29. Camp Letterman General Hospital burial ground Row 6, grave 17.
Jacob W. Herndon Co. C, 4th Tex.	20 years old. Killed July 2 and carried back to J.E. Plank's under a large locust tree towards J.S. Crawford's place and near road to Bream's Mill.
Andrew Jackson Co. G, 5th Tex.	Third Corps Hospital near road along fence under an apple tree.

S.S. Lockett
Co. E, 5th Tex.

Michael Fiscel's farm, east side of woods.

Private William L. Langley, 1st Texas, "The first man down . . . a noble, brave boy, with a minie-ball straight through the brain."

VIRGINIA

Lt. Jacob Beverage
Co. E, 31st Va.

Highland Co. Va. Under apple tree in Josiah Benner's orchard, 1 mile from Gettysburg on the state road.

Stephen Farson
Co. H, 1st Va.

With five others buried in the southwest corner of Seminary Woods.

Sgt. William H. Gaskins
Co. K, 8th Va.

Camp Letterman General Hospital burial ground on the ridge south of the hospital. Died Nov. 5, one of the last Confederates to die at Gettysburg.

John P. Hite
Co. H, 33rd Va.

Found with gold plate and teeth in upper jaw at Johnson's Div. Hospital on J.H. Picking's place about 2 1/2 miles N.E. of Gettysburg not far from the schoolhouse and near the Hunterstown Road.

Richard H. Hundley
Marmaduke Johnson's
Battery

West of McMillan's house in woods to rear of Gen. Pickett's line. Board nailed to oak tree.

Micajah McHone
Co.C, 24th Va.

N.E. corner of John Trostle's field on south bank of Rock Creek 4 miles S.E. of Gettysburg. About 40 yards east of the grave of two Mississippi soldiers.

Cpl. Joseph W. Pope
Co. G, 3rd Va.

27 years old. At F. Bream's Mill above Wm. Myers house by the side of the fence.

Sgt. William H. Prince Co. A, 5th Va.	21 years old. Killed July 3. Buried back of Culp's Hill near breastworks in woods near Union burying ground. Recovered and reburied in Stonewall Cemetery.
William A. Richerson Co. B, 9th Va. Cavalry	Age 22. North side of and close by railroad tracks 3 miles down the York Road.
Lt. Jacob G. Shoup Co. H, 7th Va. Cavalry	At Flohr's Church graveyard 8 miles up Chambersburg Pike.
Benjamin H. Stone Page's Va. Battery	Under peach tree near David Schriver's, north of house. Removed by his brother to Ashland, Hanover County, Va.
James R. Tice Co. B, 42nd Va.	North border of field back of H. Monfort's barn on the Hunterstown Road.
George W. White 2nd Rockbridge Va. Artillery	North border of E. Whistler's woods.
James H. White Co. F, 49th Va.	Killed July 3. Buried in Adams County Almshouse [Poorhouse] orchard.
Maj. Nathaniel C. Wilson 28th Va.	At John Currens' farm under a walnut tree.

Thomas F. McKie, 11th Mississippi, another who died at Gettysburg.
(Maud M. Brown)

53

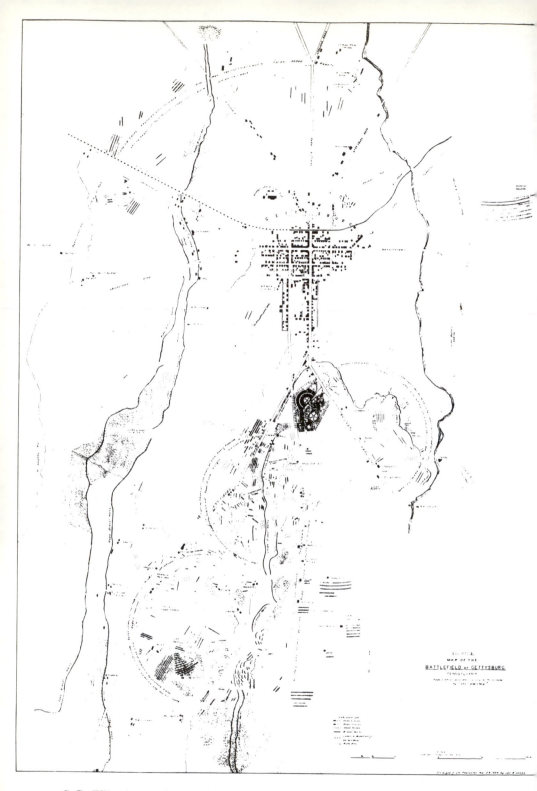

S.G. Elliott's map is very difficult to reproduce. On page 55 is a reproduction of a portion showing the Peach Orchard and Rose Farm areas.

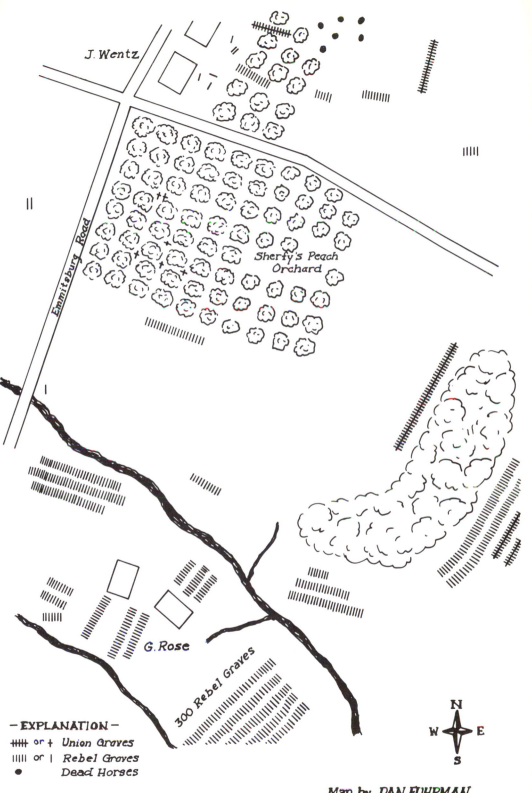

J. Wentz

Emmitsburg Road

Sherfy's Peach Orchard

G. Rose

300 Rebel Graves

— EXPLANATION —
┼┼┼┼ or ┼   Union Graves
‖‖‖ or ‖   Rebel Graves
●   Dead Horses

N
W   E
S

Map by DAN FUHRMAN

55

PART III

Farmyards, Fields and Woods; The Burial Sites

At one point, in a field at the edge of the Devil's Den woods, I found 156 Confederates buried together – that is 156 Confederates had been laid, side by side, in four parallel rows of 39 each, and a little earth had been thrown over them from different sides, through which after the ground had been settled by a heavy rain, appeared shoes, and hats, and locks of hair and portions of the bodies.[59]

J. Howard Wert
Adams County Citizen

This section, used jointly with all of the maps provided, will serve as a guide to over 120 burial locations located throughout the Gettysburg area and portions of Adams County. Within these more than one hundred sites are yet another set of positions or sub-categories, which will direct you even more precisely to the whereabouts of many of the graves of deceased Confederate soldiers. For instance, on the W.H. Monfort farm there are five distinctive places where burials were noted, one of which was "under a locust tree opposite the barn." Naturally the locust tree has long since disappeared, however, the visitor to that farm should be able to locate the barn and that may give a somewhat better impression as to where dead Southerners from Johnson's Division, as in this case, were interred.

The many sites listed in Part III were determined by using several sources. These sources were: Dr. J.W.C. O'Neal's physician's handbook, journal and letters; Dr. Rufus Weaver's letters, notes, and reports that he sent to the various women's memorial organizations which were instrumental, but did not pay for, the removal of many of the Confederate dead from the vicinity of Gettysburg; S.G. Elliott's map, plus various and miscellaneous recollections, memoirs, letters, diaries, and newspaper accounts of the period.

In the forthcoming registry, the reader might assume that each and every site is absolute and verifiable. This is, unfortunately, simply not the case.

57

Between 1863 and 1870 land ownership and land boundaries had changed, in fact drastically, in some instances. This means that if a body was noted on Douglas' farm in 1864, in 1868, farmer Slonaker now owned the land, and the few lists kept in those days often used the current landowner, not the wartime occupant. Also, in very many situations, a family legally owned a piece of property, but a tenant was living and working that particular farm, as in the example of the Nicholas Codori place along the Emmitsburg Road, southwest of town. Another problem was the overlapping of boundaries, which in its worst scenario, is readily seen in the Devil's Den-Round Top area, where within a 1,000 square yard section five or six landowners' boundaries came into contact, which makes placement of gravesites virtually impossible as to a specific farm. This occurred all over the Gettysburg battlefield locale and obviously presented great difficulties.

Lastly, the use of the S.G. Elliott map may give both the researcher and reader the most concern and frustration. Even though Elliott stated that the survey of the battlefield and its many graves was made accurately with "transit and chain," problems still arise. Gettysburg National Military Park Historian Kathy G. Harrison summed it up by saying that she almost wished the map had never been drawn, as it exposes as many problems as it solves. Apparently Elliott did come to the late battleground and did attempt to locate and mark Union and Confederate graves, and he accomplished it accurately in certain cases. But his work was not constant, and frankly in many instances it is impossible to determine where or how many graves actually existed in a given location. After studying all factors, the writer has chosen to use the map. You will notice that the text accompanying each site specifies when Elliott's estimates or gravesites are used, so that these numbers may not be taken so literally or utilized definitively.[60]

The number in parenthesis to the right of the farm name or other location is the number of Confederate bodies actually counted or witnessed at the site by O'Neal, Weaver, and others.

Collectively, all sources can and should give a good indication as to where Confederates *were* interred. And since this is a first attempt at documenting this singular aspect of the Gettysburg story, then it hopefully will stand until a better and more accurate solution comes along.

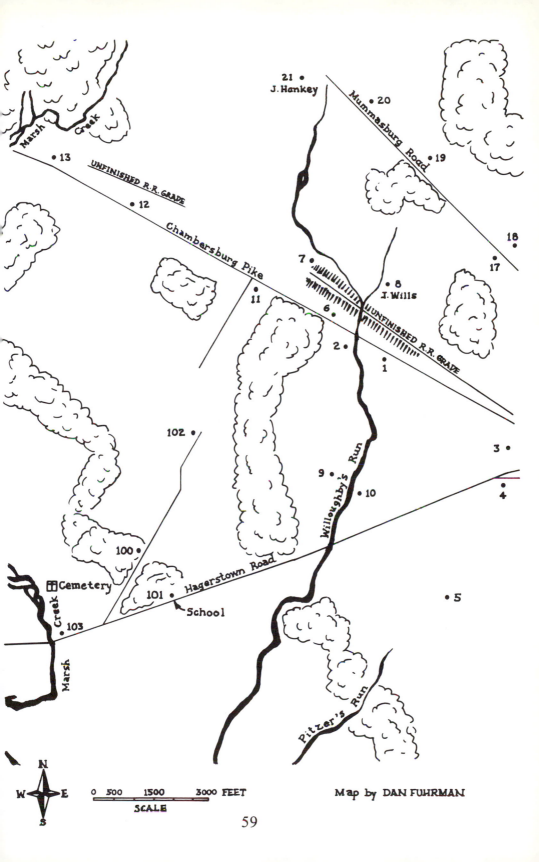

21 •
J. Hankey

• 20

Mummasburg Road

• 19

• 13

Marsh Creek

UNFINISHED R.R. GRADE

• 12

• 18

• 17

Chambersburg Pike

7 •

• 8
J. Wills

11 •

6 •

UNFINISHED R.R. GRADE

2 •

• 1

102 •

3 •

9 • Willoughby's Run

• 10

• 4

100 •

Cemetery

Hagerstown Road

101 •

School

• 5

103 •

Marsh Creek

Pitzer's Run

N
W E
S

0   500   1500   3000 FEET
SCALE

Map by DAN FUHRMAN

59

1 Edward McPherson Farm (50)

- ☞ McPherson's field to the rear of Seminary Ridge and back of the railroad cut
- ☞ left side of railroad at first cut
- ☞ on sand bar in run
- ☞ southeast of bridge over Willoughby's Run
  (Elliott's map indicates 22)
- ☞ on south side of pike, just northwest of Seminary

Fifty or more rebel graves were found along both sides of the Chambersburg Pike on Edward McPherson's land northwest of Gettysburg.

2 Willoughby's Run Vicinity* (19)

- ☞ northwest bank and under an elm tree where battle began
- ☞ south bank of run, on Fahnestock farm [1866]
  (Elliott's map indicates 57)

*These burials may have overlapped onto several farms, such as McPherson, Herr, Harman and Herbst.

3 Lutheran Theological Seminary (23)

☛ back of Charles P. Krauth house (7)

☛ to rear of Seminary toward McPherson's Ridge

☛ several bodies reported "in one hole immediately in rear of the [Seminary] building" — "exhumed to graveyard"

☛ southwest corner of Seminary Woods

The rear of the house on the Seminary campus occupied by Charles Krauth where seven Confederates were buried.

4 Elizabeth F. Schultz Farm (18)

☛ on Oak Ridge, west of Gettysburg

☛ on ridge near Mrs. Schultz's farm

☛ in orchard near Mrs. Schultz's house

☛ on Seminary Ridge near fence on Mrs. Schultz's lot

5 David McMillan Farm (5)

- 🖝 west of house in woods
- 🖝 under oak tree in rear of Pickett's line
- 🖝 west side of woods

Possible C.S. burial trenches in David McMillan's woods along Seminary Ridge.

6 John Crist Farm (5)

- 🖝 under gum tree
- 🖝 2 1/2 miles up Chambersburg Pike

7 Michael Crist Farm (3)
Pender's Division Hospital

- 🖝 under big oak tree

8 James J. Wills Farm (3)

- 🖝 north of railroad bed (Elliott's map indicates 250)
- 🖝 in first field on a ridge or "first field over ridge"

S.G. Elliott indicated over 200 rebel graves atop this knoll along the unfinished railroad bed on James Wills' farm.

9 Emmanuel Harman Farm (23)*

☛ north of farmhouse on east side of Willoughby's Run

*Elliott's map only.

10 John Herbst Farm (40)

☛ in woods where General Reynolds was killed

☛ west of Seminary Woods under elm tree
(Most from Elliott's map)

11 Frederick Herr Farm (4)

☛ south of Herr's in woods

☛ Herr's old place on turnpike; corner of garden (One soldier burial here was moved to the German Reformed Church graveyard)

☛ under large trees

☛ near house

☛ along Pike, and northwest of bridge over Willoughby's Run (Elliott's map indicates 31)

12 Charles B. Polley Farm (8)

☛ lower orchard under two apple trees

- in orchard on Chambersburg Turnpike; under white oak tree — tree is marked
- 2 1/2 miles up Chambersburg Road under gum tree near railroad
- under a walnut tree on the turnpike — 100 yards from the road in a field — "under a walnut tree . . . on the north side of the turnpike road — 75 yards NE of a medium-sized stone farm house, which has a large yellow barn on the opposite side of the road"
- ". . . under a tree, in a large field near a stone house . . ."

13 Ephraim Whisler Farm and Blacksmith Shop (7)

- west of house in woods bottom — "blaze on tree"
- northeast corner of barn under apple tree
- north border of Whisler's woods
- at blacksmith shop on Chambersburg Road
- in woods toward creek
- left of Whisler's shop in edge of woods
- right of Whisler's shop
- near woods

14 Samuel Lohr Farm (66)
Heth's Division Hospital

- in woods, north side
- opposite the house in meadow
- on east side of house under a pear tree

This meadow used as a graveyard, was opposite Mr. Lohr's old farmhouse.

15 Andrew Heintzelman Tavern and Farm (92)
Pender's Division Hospital

☞ east of tavern near peach tree

16 Isaac Rife Farm (2)

☞ under chestnut tree

17 John S. Forney Farm (70)
Rodes' Division Hospital

☞ in field under apple tree

☞ at foot of Forney's garden

☞ in field to rear of Confederate left center (64)

The so-called "Iverson's Pits" were located in one of Forney's fields southeast of the house. One eyewitness said 79 rebels were buried there. (Elliott's map indicates over 170 graves here.)

The scene where "Iverson's Pits" were dug on John Forney's farm northwest of town.

18 Moses McClean Farm (19)

☞ southwest of house along the lane in the cherry thicket

☞ south, in meadow
(Elliott's map indicates approximately 35 on this farm.)

19 Jacob Hershey Farm (1)

☞ northwest corner of orchard

Mr. Hershey's farmhouse on Herr's Ridge where the lonely grave of Captain W.T. Palmore, 3rd Alabama, lay for almost 10 years.

20 David Schriver Farm (16)
Rodes' Division Hospital

☞ north of house in corner of orchard

☞ under peach tree north of house in corner of orchard

21 Jacob Hankey Farm (145)
Iverson's and Daniels' Brigade Hospital

☞ under a peach tree

22 Pennsylvania College (35)
Early's Division Hospital

☞ north side of main building

23 John S. Crawford House (2)

☞ north of brick house - near Harrisburg Road

☞ back of brick house towards Almshouse along fence

Looking north past Schriver's stone house to where at least sixteen Southerners were buried in the orchard.

The north side of the college edifice became the last resting place for many of Early's Confederates.

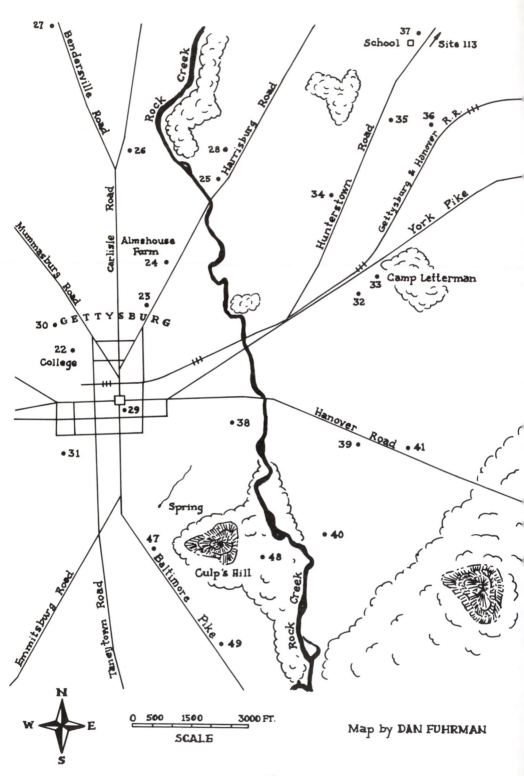

27 •

Bendersville Road

Rock Creek

37 •
School ☐ // Site 113

• 26

28 •

Harrisburg Road

25 •

• 35   36 •

Gettysburg & Hanover R.R.

Hunterstown Road

34 •

York Pike

Carlisle Road

Almshouse Farm
24 •

Mummasburg Road

Camp Letterman

33 •
32 •

23 •

30 • GETTYSBURG

22 •
College

• 29

• 38

Hanover Road • 41

39 •

• 31

Spring

47 •

• 40

Culp's Hill

• 48

Baltimore Pike

Emmitsburg Road

Taneytown Road

Rock Creek

• 49

N
W ✦ E
S

0 500   1500   3000 FT.
SCALE

Map by DAN FUHRMAN

24 Adams County Almshouse (9)

- ☞ under wild cherry tree at northeast border of Gettysburg
- ☞ in orchard
- ☞ north of Almshouse under walnut tree near graveyard
- ☞ in Almshouse burying house
- ☞ on hill back of graveyard
- ☞ field under tree on Carlisle Road
- ☞ under apple tree near road

25 Josiah Benner Farm (25)

- ☞ in orchard
- ☞ in meadow along fence
- ☞ under swamp oak near creek
- ☞ under a large walnut tree
- ☞ northeast of Blocher's Hill [Barlow's Knoll] (Elliott's map indicates 21)

26 David Blocher Farm (2)

- ☞ under a tree near house
- ☞ northeast of house, behind barn
- ☞ southeast of farm buildings (Elliott's map indicates 28)

27 Samuel Cobean Farm (1)

- ☞ west of house in woods along Poorhouse [Almshouse] fence

28 Jacob Kime Farm (14)
Gordon's Brigade Hospital

- ☞ in orchard under peach tree

29 Borough of Gettysburg (5)

- ☞ old Presbyterian Graveyard (2) in the northwest area of Gettysburg, at North Street and Washington Street
- ☞ south side of brick house at east end of Middle Street (Henry Culp house) (2)
- ☞ Fahnestock brother's lot — at corner of barn near or toward Miller's house (1)
- ☞ behind or southeast of brickyard in southern outskirts of Gettysburg (Elliott's map indicates 32)

Elliott's map lists the grave of James M. Williams, 6th North Carolina Infantry, about 1/8 mile east of the railroad depot and just north of the tracks.

30 Adam Doersom Farm (3)

☞ in meadow

31 The Negro Church (2)

☞ opposite church on Long Lane

☞ Long Lane beyond colored church

☞ negro graveyard outside fence

The old Negro Graveyard where William Butler, 4th Georgia, was interred. The church stood along Long Lane which is in the background.

32 George Wolf Farm (17)

☞ northeast of farm under pin oak near gatehouse on York Pike

☞ along edge of Hospital Woods — graves destroyed by General Hospital grounds

☞ General Hospital yard

33 U.S. General Hospital (Camp Letterman)* (181)

☛ General Hospital burial yard and edge of woods

☛ behind hospital, south, on ridge
One nurse there stated that approximately 400 Southerners were buried here.

*There were at least 9 rows of Confederate graves in the hospital cemetery.

The scene westward across the general hospital burial ground at Camp Letterman. The camp was off to the right.

34 W. Henry Monfort Farm (52)

Johnson's Division Hospital

☛ under locust tree opposite barn

☛ southeast corner of field back of barn

☛ north border of field back of barn

☛ under apple tree in orchard

☛ under apple tree along road above house

One of Henry Monfort's fields west of the barn where some of Johnson's casualties were consigned to the grave.

35 Martin Shealer Farm* (21)
Steuart's Brigade Hospital

- ☛ under apple tree in orchard
- ☛ in meadow next to Mrs. E. Weible
- ☛ under little apple tree

*One source noted 44 Confederate burials here behind the barn.

36 Elizabeth Weible Farm (13)
Steuart's Brigade Hospital

- ☛ back of barn
- ☛ near York Road in fence corner above house
- ☛ below house in fence corner

37 Henry A. Picking Farm (16)
Walker's Brigade Hospital

- ☛ not far from schoolhouse and near the Hunterstown Road
- ☛ under apple tree above house near road
- ☛ in field along fence opposite the schoolhouse

Looking to the rear of Martin Shealer's barn where it was said over forty rebels were buried.

Mr. Picking's field across from the schoolhouse which held the bodies of some of the old "Stonewall Brigade."

38 Henry Culp Farm (33)
Co-owned by Peter Raffensberger

- ☞ in orchard under apple tree
- ☞ Culp's field near Gettysburg
- ☞ southeast of Culp's Hill (Elliott's map indicates 189)
- ☞ south side of brick house

Please note that many more burials occurred on the farm but are listed under "Culp's Hill."

39 David Benner Farm (4)

40 Christian Benner Farm (6)

- ☞ in orchard
- ☞ back of Rock Creek under a large walnut tree

41 Daniel Lady Farm (8)
Jones' Brigade Hospital

- ☞ back of barn
- ☞ near stone house on south side of Hanover Road
- ☞ near barn

One of the burial plots on Daniel Lady's farm was just opposite his substantial stone dwelling.

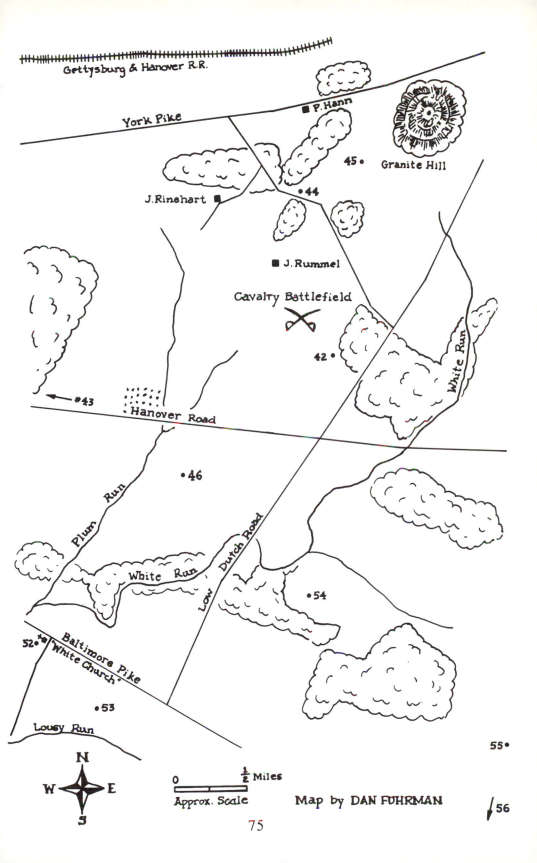

Gettysburg & Hanover R.R.

York Pike

■ P. Hann

Granite Hill

45 •

• 44

J. Rinehart ■

■ J. Rummel

Cavalry Battlefield

42 •

White Run

#43

Hanover Road

• 46

Plum Run

White Run

Low Dutch Road

• 54

52 •■
Baltimore Pike
White Church

• 53

Lousy Run

55 •

N
W   E
S

0   ½ Miles
Approx. Scale

Map by DAN FUHRMAN

56

75

42 Jacob Lott Farm (5)
Stuart's Cavalry Division Hospital

43 Jacob Brinkerhoff Farm (2)
Stuart's Cavalry Division Hospital

44 Isaac Miller Farm* (1)
Stuart's Cavalry Division Hospital

*There was a tannery on this farm in 1863.

Isaac Miller's farm in Stuart's rear became a field hospital and was the last stop for some of his cavalrymen.

45 Joseph B. Leas Farm (6)
Stuart's Cavalry Division Hospital

- ☛ northwest corner of field
- ☛ along the north side of the railroad and close by the tracks
- ☛ west of house, in corner of field
- ☛ northwest of Leas farm on railroad near P. Hann's

This ground on Joseph Leas' farm held more of JEB Stuart's men killed or mortally wounded on July 3.

46 Abraham Tawney Farm (1)

- ☞ in graveyard nearby

47 Cemetery Hill Area* (3)

- ☞ east side of hill
- ☞ west of gatehouse
- ☞ at foot of hill and north of Raffensberger's Spring
  (Elliott's map indicates 46 burials east of the hill.)

*Two Confederates who died at Jacob Schwartz's farm were later buried in Evergreen Cemetery in 1866-67.

48 Culp's Hill* Vicinity (26)

NOTE: This area encompassed the Henry Culp/Abraham Spangler/ James McKnight farms. Most of the Confederate burials appear to be in the southeast section of Culp's farm and the northeast section of Spangler's farm. Please see Culp and Spangler for specific sites.

*Culp's Hill at one time prior to the war was locally known as Raspberry Hill.

The low ground below the Union breastworks leading up to Culp's Hill was filled with long, deep burial trenches; one visitor counted at least seventeen.

49 Abraham Spangler Farm* (5)
Baltimore Pike

- ☛ under gum tree
- ☛ north corner of field by the side of the woods
- ☛ Spangler's woods back of Culp's Hill
- ☛ back of hill near breastworks from Union burying ground
- ☛ by Union graves

*This farm was actually owned by the father, Abraham, but was worked by the son, Henry. Please note that many burials occurred on this farm but are located under "Culp's Hill."

50 James McAllister Farm and Mills (3)

- ☛ west of the dam on Rock Creek and in sight of the Baltimore Pike (Elliott's map indicates 3 also)

51 Isaac M. Diehl Farm (1)

- ☛ to the rear of the barn

52 Mark's German Reformed or "White Church" (2)
U.S. 1st Division, First Corps Hospital

- ☛ graveyard

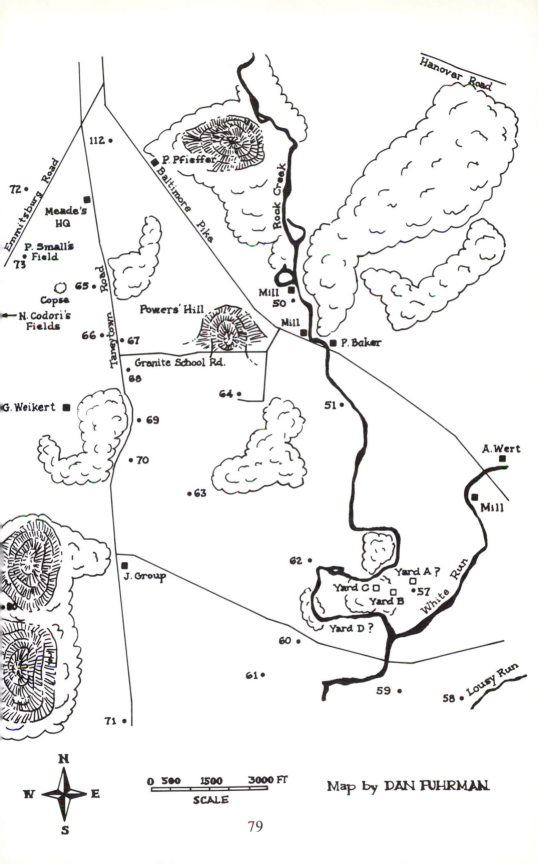

Hanover Road

112 •

Emmitsburg Road

72 •

P. Pfieffer

Rock Creek

Meade's HQ

Baltimore Pike

P. Small's Field
73

65 •
Copse

N. Codori's Fields

Powers' Hill

66 • • 67

Taneytown Road

Granite School Rd.
68 •

64 •

Mill
50

Mill

P. Baker

51 •

G. Weikert

• 69

A. Wert

• 70

Mill

• 63

J. Group

62 •

Yard A ?

Yard C □   □ • 57
Yard B

White Run

Yard D ?

60 •

61 •

59 •   58 • Lousy Run

71 •

N
W   E
S

0 500   1500   3000 FT
SCALE

Map by DAN FUHRMAN

79

The "White Church" graveyard which surrounded the little burial plot of Edgar Hammond, 1st Maryland Battalion.

53 Peter Conover Farm (5)

U.S. 2nd Division, First Corps Hospital

☛ south of house at edge of woods

54 Jonathan Young Farm (1)

U.S. 3rd Division, First Corps Hospital

☛ near the Pike

55 Samuel Durboraw Farm (2)

These burials were also listed on the Jonathan Young farm which was adjacent.

56 Jesse Worley Farm (7)

U.S. 3rd Division, Fifth Corps Hospital

57 Jacob Schwartz Farm* (257)

U.S. Second and Third Corps Hospital

☛ yard or Cemetery B — between Schwartz's and Bushman's

☛ yard or Cemetery D — in cornfield

☛ yard or Cemetery C — in woods on hill above creek

☛ at barn or back of barn

- ground between Schwartz's and Bushman's
- in cornfield on Rock Creek — along lane under walnut tree near creek
- west of house near bank of the creek in woods on "Red Hill" (Yard C)
- on hill between Schwartz's and Bushman's under a walnut tree

*One report noted that 192 rebels died in this hospital. J.H. Wert says he saw 500 of the rebels laid in rows on the high ground overlooking Rock Creek. This is probably an exaggeration.

Original but now empty graves still visible on Jacob Schwartz's old farm overlooking Rock Creek.

The area behind Schwartz's bank barn where so many Confederates were laid to rest.

One of several burial yards was here on the banks of White Run west of Mr. Schwartz's farm buildings.

58 Michael Fiscel Farm (12)

U.S. Fifth Corps Hospital

- ☞ east side of woods
- ☞ east of house across the creek or branch
- ☞ Third Corps area near road along fence under an apple tree
- ☞ at the edge of a woods

The hospital graveyard on the Fiscel farm was several hundred yards east of the house and across a small creek called Lousy Run.

59 John Trostle Farm (11)

U.S. Sixth Corps Hospital

- ☞ northeast corner of field on south bank of Rock Creek
- ☞ 40 yards east of above
- ☞ northwest corner of field on north bank of Rock Creek
- ☞ north branch of creek in field

60 Henry Beitler Tenant House* (1)

- ☞ south side of house at corner of woods

*The tenant here was probably Michael Diener.

The few Confederates who died on John Trostle's farm were mainly buried north of the barn on the south bank of Rock Creek.

Lt. Iowa Michigan Royster, 37th North Carolina, was very likely interred near this ancient sycamore tree on Rock Creek at Trostle's.

61 Lewis A. Bushman Farm (8)

☛ southeast of farmhouse
(Elliott's map indicates 8, which may extend onto the Henry Beitler tenant site.)

62 George Bushman Farm (30)
U.S. Twelfth Corps Hospital

☛ north of house/barn

☛ Bushman's, on McMullin's side [1868]

63 Jacob Swisher Farm* (6)

☛ northwest corner of field near county road

☛ opposite John Group's farm across road on [Swisher's] farm

*This farm of 143 acres was owned by Swisher until several months after the battle when it was sold to Messers Buehler and Eichelberger. Swisher then moved to a 59 acre farm on the Taneytown Road.

64 George Spangler Farm (4)
U.S. Eleventh Corps Hospital

65 Peter Frey Farm (1)

☛ in orchard

☛ close by breastworks and near Meade's Headquarters at the "Angle" (Elliott's map indicates 80)

☛ north and west of farm building (Elliott's map indicates 34)

*These may overlap onto adjacent properties.

66 Jacob Hummelbaugh Farm (2)

☛ "in front of the house"

☛ "near the . . . house, . . . under a cherry tree south of the lane"

67 William Patterson Farm (24)*

☛ east and south of farm buildings and east side of Taneytown Road
*Elliott's map only

68 Michael Frey Farm (1)

☛ northwest of the Eleventh Corps Hospital, east of the Taneytown Road. Elliott's map places Frey's farm in the wrong location.

69 John Musser Farm (26)*

*Elliott's map only

70 Sarah Patterson Farm (7)*

☞ southeast of house and road

*Elliott's map only

71 Jacob Weikert Farm (35)*

☞ across or northeast of the Taneytown Road and opposite the farm buildings

☞ just south of Little Round Top

*Elliott's map only

72 William Bliss Farm (200)*

☞ along Emmitsburg Road and east of burned farm buildings

*Elliott's map only

73 Pius A. Small Farm* (300)**

*Small's fields were directly in front of the "Angle." He may have been the tenant at the N. Codori farm in 1863.

**Elliott's map only

Pius Small's field north of Codori's house and west of the "Angle" held the graves of over a hundred Southern soldiers killed on July 3.

74 Nicholas Codori Farm* (583)

- ☞ "south side of Codori's barn"
- ☞ front of house on the Confederate line from Sherfy's
- ☞ west side of farm
- ☞ west of barn
- ☞ near edge of woods
- ☞ on the east side of the Emmitsburg Road, just inside the fence and near the south end of Codori's barn

*Many of the 583 were actually buried in P.A. Small's field north of Codori's.

75 Peter Rogers Farm (1)

- ☞ in a field behind the house
  (Elliott's map indicates about 10 in the vicinity.)

76 Henry Spangler Farm* (48)**
Emmitsburg Road

- ☞ mostly north and northeast of farm buildings

*This farm was occupied during the battle by tenant, Jacob C. Eckenrode (age 24) and his wife, Nancy Keckler (age 15)

**Elliott's map only

77 Joseph Sherfy Farm (1)

Dr. Rufus Weaver supposedly left 40 Confederates buried in Sherfy's peach orchard which were never collected or shipped to Richmond.

77a John Wentz Farm (?)

- ☞ "trench in garden to the left and in front of house near the road"

78 Peter Trostle Farm* (13)**

- ☞ south of Emmitsburg Road and near peach orchard

*This farm was actually owned by Abraham's father, Peter, although it is usually known by the son's name.

**Elliott's map indicates over 100 burials on this farm in the northwest sections, and overlapping onto D. Klingle's farm.

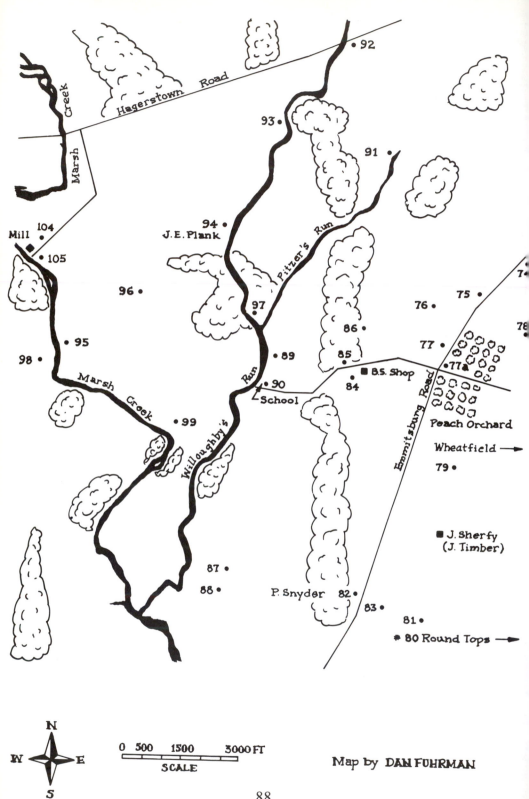

Map by DAN FUHRMAN

79 George Rose Farm (238)*

This farm was owned by Dorothy and George Rose who apparently lived part of the year in Germantown, Pa., where they were originally from, and where George worked as a butcher. His brother John, a drover, probably actually operated the farm on a day-to-day basis. Both George and John filed for Federal damage claims after the battle, each stating that at least "1000 rebels" were buried on the farm; 100 in the garden, 175 behind the barn and around the wagon shed, and a colonel interred within "one yard of the kitchen door." [possibly Lt. Col. Francis Kearse, 50th Ga. Inf.]

Within several years after the war, J. H. Wert wrote that he was told that "1500" bodies had been buried on the Rose property. As can be seen with each passing year, the number of burials began to rise, and the horror was magnified with each retelling of the story.

- in orchard near fence
- north and back of barn
- under pear tree
- northwest of Rose's and north of Emmitsburg Road along fence near some trees
- west of barn under large cherry tree

This present day photograph was taken in the same location on the George Rose farm as the 1863 cover photo for this book. For a complete description see the section entitled "Photo Acknowledgements."

89

- south of Rose's house, edge of woods
- in orchard near fence and springhouse
- opposite Rose's house near a pear tree
- across the "road in the timothy field"
- near "grave-walk in the woods" between the apple trees and the washhouse
- under an apple tree near the meadow stream
- in woods opposite the wheatfield
- in the meadow, peach orchard
- in garden, then moved to ridge 1/2 mile east of the house (10)

*Many of these burials overlap onto G. Weikert's property and J. Sherfy's (where J.W. Timber lived).

Looking north, back of the Rose barn where many Confederates were interred during and shortly after the battle.

This area east of Rose's house was filled with the graves of rebels killed on July 2.

A famous photograph of Confederate dead in the vicinity of the Rose farm.

Due to the complexity of land ownership in this vicinity, it was difficult to pinpoint on whose farms most of the Confederates were buried. Farms or land which overlapped the Round Top or Devil's Den sites were owned by P. Snyder, J. Slyder, G. Rose, J. Houck, E. Hanaway, H.G. Scott, J. Guinn, J. Weikert and J. Sherfy. For instance, on the land of John Houck east of and along Plum Run, Elliott's map indicates over 200 rebel graves.

80 The Round Tops and Devil's Den Areas (103)

- ☞ around Devil's Den
- ☞ ridge north of Round Top
- ☞ in the swamp
- ☞ across and near the edge of the swamp. (Those *in* the swamp had been washed away.)
- ☞ in gap between Big and Little Round Tops
- ☞ at the edge of the Devil's Den woods (159 here reported by an eyewitness — these may be a portion which show up on the George Rose farm)

81 John Slyder Farm (5)

- ☞ near barn
- ☞ under a cherry tree
- ☞ back of barn, 2 rows

(Elliott's map indicates over 100 which overlapped somewhat onto the farms of H. Scott and J. Guinn, and P. Snyder)

Back of John Slyder's barn where "two rows" of Southerners were buried.

82 Philip Snyder Farm (6)

☛ "several here" reported by Samuel Weaver
(Elliott's map indicates 6)

83 Michael Bushman Farm (10)

☛ to rear of Confederate breastworks, extreme right, northeast of Emmitsburg Road, under a large oak tree. These may overlap onto the Currens and Douglas farms.
(Elliott's map indicates 12 graves)

84 James Warfield Farm and Blacksmith Shop (14)

☛ in garden near blacksmith shop in front of Confederate line of fortifications

☛ near Negro blacksmith shop on road to Mr. Krise's near peach orchard

☛ right side of shop

☛ northwest corner of barn
(Elliott's map indicates approximately 13)

85 Christian Shefferer Farm* (3)

☛ close by Mr. Schefferer's barn . . . near Emmitsburg Road and close by Longstreet's line

☛ at Christian Schaefferer farm on Eckert's Mill Road

☛ corner of [Schaefferer's] Farm near school

*spelling varies — Schafferer, Schefferer, Schaefferer, etc.

86 John Straub Farm (23)*

*Elliott's map only

87 John Biesecker Farm* (20)**

*Currently a part of the Eisenhower National Historic Site

**Elliott's map only

88 William Douglas Farm* (12)
Emmitsburg Road

(Elliott's map indicates 31 which may overlap onto A. Currens farm)

*Currently a part of the Eisenhower National Historic Site

89 Samuel Pitzer Farm (29)

☛ south of S. Pitzer's in edge of woods near Joe Myers' land [1866]

☛ in woods south of Pitzer's and west of J. Socks' near a run or dry

water course

☛ on road to Mr. Krise's in woods between Pitzer's and blacksmith shop

☛ Pitzer's place back of Myers' [1866] lot and above the garden

☛ east end of Pitzer's woods

☛ near county road at handboard that stands between Pitzer's and Socks' under wild cherry tree

☛ under pin oak in Pitzer's woods

☛ under apple tree in orchard

☛ woods, in rear of Confederate right center

On Pitzer's farm looking northwest - his fields were dotted with rebel graves.

90 Pitzer's Schoolhouse Vicinity (5)

☛ in woods on road to Krise's near Schoolhouse

☛ in woods on road from Plank's to Pitzer's Schoolhouse near a log house on Willoughby's Run

☛ near Schoolhouse, on road to Krise's in field near fence

☛ in woods near Pitzer's School near little house

☛ corner of . . . farm near school

91 Emmanuel Pitzer Farm (17)

- ☛ in orchard near George Culp's
- ☛ above the garden
- ☛ east of house in meadow under peach tree
- ☛ south of house in edge of woods

92 John Horting Farm* (10)
Davis' Brigade Hospital

- ☛ on bluff along Willoughby's Run
- ☛ under a walnut tree in southeast corner of garden
- ☛ "near the garden fence"

*This farm was owned by George Arnold.

93 George Culp Farm (8)
Hood's Division Hospital

- ☛ near Willoughby's Run

94 John Edward Plank Farm (118)
Hood's Division Hospital

- ☛ under pin oaks

The ground north of J.E. Plank's brick house where some of the men that Hood's surgeons couldn't save were laid to rest.

- north of house under walnut tree
- under white oak
- back of barn (32)
- south of house in orchard under apple tree
- under tree right and front of house toward Millerstown Road and Gettysburg
- under a large locust tree toward Crawford's place and near road to Bream's Mill
- foot of garden near road; garden fence runs over the grave

95 John S. Crawford Farm (45)
Barksdale's Brigade Hospital

- "Walnut Avenue," north side under apple tree
- in garden (22)
- at head of the road under walnut tree
- under walnut tree east of house
- in orchard (11)
- Crawford's, in garden where Basil Biggs lives
- under tree on road from mansion to tenant house
- corner of woods, back of Socks, under a white oak tree near the fence

96 Samuel Johns House (10)

- southeast of tenant barn
- Crawford's tenant house near barn in field
- Crawford's tenant house where Johns lives
- east of Johns' tenant house
- in woods east of house
- east of barn at Johns'

97 S.A. Felix Farm (2)

- near house on left side of county road towards S. Pitzer's
- near S.A. Felix's house along road on left side going to S. Pitzer's under a locust or walnut tree in the field where the road makes a turn going to the tenant house

98 John Cunningham Farm (14)
Wofford's Brigade Hospital

- ☞ in orchard on a hill between farm and Scott's place
- ☞ two rows of Confederate graves in a "sunny corner of the orchard"
- ☞ orchard, southside

The hill where John Cunningham carefully tended the Confederate graves in the southern corner of his orchard.

99 John Socks Farm (15)

- ☞ near barn on Marsh Creek
- ☞ along side of barn

100 Adam Butt Farm (27)
Wilcox's Brigade Hospital

- ☞ north of house under cherry tree
- ☞ west of house at the road in corner of woods
- ☞ Butt's woods, south of house near the road toward Bream's

101 Butt's Schoolhouse (10)
Wright's Brigade Hospital

- ☞ at the brick schoolhouse on Millerstown [Fairfield] Road

The burial area near John Sock's barn on Marsh Creek, with his large house in the background.

102 Dr. Samuel E. Hall Farm (2)

☞ east of Dr. Hall's place in woods near county road

Two Confederates from Pettigrew's Brigade were buried east of Dr. Hall's stone house, which is to the left across the road.

103 Francis Bream's Farm (Black Horse Tavern) (20)
Kershaw's Brigade Hospital

- ☛ north of house on hill, at edge of woods
- ☛ north of Bream's in field near woods along side of A. Butt's woods near road
- ☛ Bream's, at McClellan's private burying ground (The William McClellan family had previously owned this farm.)
- ☛ in Bream's orchard
- ☛ north of Bream's tavern on Marsh Creek near burial place
- ☛ in Bream's burial ground, center

The hill north of Bream's "Black Horse" Tavern where many of General Kershaw's finest soldiers were interred.

The old McClellan family cemetery in Cumberland Township.

104 John F. Currens Farm (34)

Pickett's Division Hospital

- ☛ southeast of house, in orchard
- ☛ northeast of house, corner of field in edge of woods on south bank of Bream's Mill dam
- ☛ southwest of house — row of graves
- ☛ west of house, corner of garden
- ☛ back of Currens' near Bream's Mill dam
- ☛ at Currens' under walnut tree
- ☛ in garden

One of the burial sites on Curren's farm which held the remains of Pickett's men. This one southwest of the house had "a row of graves."

105 Francis Bream's Mill (18)

Pickett's Division Hospital

- ☛ above William E. Myers' house at mill by the side of fence (Myers was the master miller and lived next to the mill.)
- ☛ at the dam
- ☛ in woods across creek from mill
- ☛ on the hill across from Bream's Mill

Here is "the hill across from Bream's Mill" where more of Pickett's men lie.

The woods across the creek from the mill.

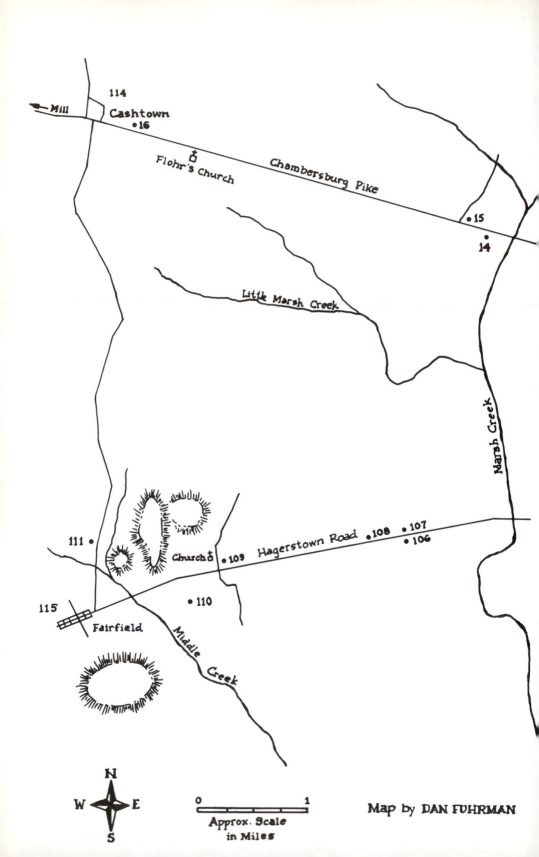

114

→ Mill

Cashtown
•16

Flohr's Church

Chambersburg Pike

•15

•14

Little Marsh Creek

Marsh Creek

111 •

Hagerstown Road   •108   •107
                            •106

Church ☗   •109

•110

115

Fairfield

Middle Creek

N
W — E
S

0 — 1
Approx. Scale
in Miles

Map by DAN FUHRMAN

106 Jacob Plank Farm (36)
Daniels' Brigade Hospital

- ☞ under walnut tree near road
- ☞ east of barn
- ☞ back of barn — "graves plowed over"

107 Christian Byers Farm (3)
Hoke's Brigade Hospital

108 Andrew Weikert Farm (22)
Gordon's Brigade Hospital

109 William Douglas Farm (2)
Fairfield Road

- ☞ northeast corner of orchard under apple tree

110 David Stewart Farm (15)

- ☞ east of barn and near row of trees
- ☞ in woods near the barn

111 Benjamin A. Marshall Farm (6)
Fairfield area

- ☞ in corner of orchard
- ☞ under locust tree near the house

112 Soldiers' National Cemetery (10)
See Appendix D for names and locations

113 · Hunterstown Area (8)

- ☞ corner of John A. Felty's field under cherry tree
- ☞ under cherry tree near Hunterstown on Hunterstown Road
- ☞ Presbyterian Graveyard

114 Cashtown Area (10)

- ☞ Flohr's Church graveyard
- ☞ near Cashtown
- ☞ at sawmill two miles up mountain above Cashtown
- ☞ at Latshaw Farm [1866]

115 Fairfield (Millerstown) Area (16)

- ☞ at Reed's place at the foot of South Mountain, 2 miles above Millerstown

☞ at gatehouse above Monterey Springs

116 Hanover Area (2)

☞ near Karl Forney House by the road near a fence under a locust tree. This was about 100 yards southwest of Hanover's old city limits.

☞ near barn on Martin Arnold farm, north of Conewago Hill near blacksmith shop along Westminster Road, 3 miles south of town in the Gitt's Mill area

117 Westminster, Maryland Area (2)

☞ Union Church yard

118 Chambersburg Area (1)

☞ Methodist Church graveyard

119 McConnellsburg Area (3)

☞ just inside Daniel Fore's meadow along the Mercersburg Pike

120 Emmitsburg, Maryland (2)

☞ Grotto

121 Hagerstown, Maryland

☞ Confederate Cemetery, "Rose Hill."

John Felty's barn southwest of Hunterstown near where several Southern officers and enlisted men were interred.

McClellan's Cemetery where Col. DeSaussure was first buried after his death at Bream's Tavern.

Raffensberger's Spring southeast of Cemetery Hill near where Captain Gray's remains were found by his father and carried home.

PART IV

A Fearful Verification: The Men, Their Stories, Their Deaths

Every grave had its history, and thousands were there.[61]
Sophronia E. Bucklin
Volunteer nurse at Gettysburg

[The rebels] boasted that in coming into [Pennsylvania] they had got back into the Union - many who thus boasted occupied those [burial] trenches. Their boasting had met a fearful verification.[62]
Jacob Hoke
Chambersburg, Pa. Citizen

. . . the dead are laid out in long rows, with their naked faces turned up to the sun, their clothes stiff with the dried blood, and their features retaining in death the agony and pain which they died with; and presently they are dragged forth and thrust into a shallow pit, with, perhaps, the coarse jest of a vulgar soldier for their requiem, and bloody blankets for their winding sheets.[63]
Captain D. et U. Barziza
4th Texas Infantry

Often while collecting research on the Confederate burials at Gettysburg, some personal narrative would surface, covering a specific soldier who was killed during the battle, or who died of wounds hours, days, or weeks later. Out of approximately 160 narratives assembled, fifty were chosen to include within these pages. These fifty compiled biographies are, of course, only a small number of the over 4,500 Southerners who died as a result of that battle. Their intimate stories of anguish, death, and courage were usually recalled and written by comrades, military nurses, surgeons, the Union captors, and civilians.

The purpose here is to emphasize the human aspect of men suffering and dying far from home, who were now in the hands of the enemy. The impact of seeing as many as 5,000 dead or dying soldiers collectively is too overwhelming to comprehend — one must see them as individuals, as people. It would seem more equitable to let every man be recognized and to

107

have had a friend, or even a stranger, to recall their last moments. But unfortunately, that was not possible. Hopefully, these accounts will impart some notion of the price of the folly of war.

⚜

Colonel John A. Jones, 20th Georgia Infantry

General Henry L. Benning reported that on July 2 near the Devil's Den, "Colonel Jones was killed late in the action, not far from the captured guns, after the enemy's forces were driven from the position and they had themselves opened upon it with shell from their own batteries, a fragment of one which, glancing from a rock, passed through his brain. He had behaved with great coolness and gallantry."

One of Jones's own men, Private J.W. Lokey of Company B, also saw the colonel, probably shortly after he was killed. His simple description was much more to the point.

"I advanced up the hill to the right. In ascending to the right I passed Col. Jack Jones, of my regiment, lying on his back with about half of his head shot off."

Dr. J.W.C. O'Neal's journal of 1868 states that several officers, one "of apparent rank and refinement," were buried back of the barn on the John Slyder farm. Three years earlier in December of 1865, Samuel Weaver recalled this while writing to a Mrs. Bedinger who was searching for her husband, Captain George R. Bedinger, 33rd Virginia:

> . . . a few days ago I got a letter from Mrs. Jones of Columbus Ga, saying to me that Col. Jones fell while making a charge on little Round Top - on [the] Snyder farm & was buried about 150 yds. from the house under a cherry tree & was wounded in through the left side of his head. I went out to examine the graves on Mr. Snyder's farm but I couldent find such a location as she described on Mr. Snyder's place. I then went on the next farm a Mr. Slyder. There I found a cherry tree about 150 yds. from the house with two graves under it. I opened them both and in the one I found the remains of a soldier to answer the descriptions Mrs. Jones sent me, wounded in the left side of his head and the left lower jaw broken.

Mrs. Jones evidently arranged to have the colonel shipped home by Mr. Weaver. Unfortunately on the way south to Savannah the ship was lost at sea, and Colonel Jones's remains probably now rest in a watery grave off the eastern shore of the United States.[64]

Private Marshall Prue, 5th Texas Infantry

This young Texan was one of the fifty plus men of the 5th Texas who was killed or mortally wounded on July 2 in General Jerome Robertson's attack on the Houck's Ridge area just west of Little Round Top. Ironically, Prue was one of the few casualties anywhere on the battlefield whose grave was

108

noted by two separate visitors.

Andrew B. Cross, a member of the U.S. Christian Commission, visited the battleground about July 7 and saw, ". . . below the rocks, in the lower part of a meadow, on the other side, also alone, is Marshal Prue, Company F, 5th Texas — A piece of rail . . . was driven in at the head of the grave, and the name written with a lead pencil."

Edward Bird, a Baltimore resident, apparently viewed the same area on Monday, August 24. After walking over the George Rose farm, Bird observed this:

"Way down in one corner of a field and near the base of the Round Top, was the grave of a Texan soldier named M. Prue, 5th Texas, his old coat was lieing alongside of his grave."

Regrettably, even as early as 1866 this grave was no longer recorded by Dr. O'Neal, and during the removals by Dr. Rufus Weaver in the summers of 1871, 1872, and 1873, his body was not included with those shipped to the South for reinterment. It had become just another lost grave, wiped off the face of the earth by weathering, or the carelessness or vandalism of some battlefield visitor.[65]

Lieutenant Henry A. Rauch, 14th South Carolina Infantry

Georgeanna Woolsey, a volunteer nurse at Gettysburg for three weeks, worked at the U.S. Sanitary Commission Relief Lodge located adjacent to the railroad depot on Carlisle Street. On July 16, a Confederate soldier was brought there in an ambulance from one of the field hospitals to await his turn for transportation to Baltimore. She recalled that he was a "fair-haired, blue-eyed young Lieutenant" who was weak and faint, badly hurt and failing - very near death. Ms. Woolsey took a special interest in the man, coaxing him to take some nourishment and talked with him for several hours during the night. She identified the rebel as Lt. Rauch and related how he said that his father was old and ailing, and was a Lutheran clergyman in South Carolina. She later wrote:

"All day long we watched him - sometimes fighting his battles over - oftever singing his Lutheran chants - till in at the tent door, close to which he lay, looked a rebel soldier, just arrived with other prisoners."

This soldier knew Rauch, and told Woolsey that the lieutenant's brother was also wounded, and was in one of the prison train cars now. Soon, the brothers were reunited. Henry Rauch, however, was sinking fast and did not recognize his brother who stayed by him until evening. Ms. Woolsey continued:

> And there the brothers lay, and there we, strangers, sat watching, and listening to the strong clear voice, singing, 'Lord, have mercy upon me.' The Lord had mercy, and at sunset [July 17] I put my hand on the Lieutenant's heart to find it still!
>
> All night the brother lay close against the coffin, and in the morning he went away with his comrades, leaving us to bury Henry . . . giving us

all that he had to show his gratitude - the palmetto ornament from his brother's cap and a button from his coat.

Dr. W. read the burial service that morning at the grave, and wrote his name on the little headboard.

Lieutenant Rauch was evidently interred in Adam Doersom's "meadow" which was on the northwestern edge of Gettysburg about 600 yards from the railroad station. In 1866 Dr. O'Neal noted this grave as still well-marked and in good condition.[66]

Private J.W. Shackelfore, 9th Louisiana Infantry

This soldier was very likely the first Confederate to be buried in the Gettysburg area. Dr. J.W.C. O'Neal, the local physician originally from Fairfax County, Virginia, who had moved to Adams County in February 1863 told the following story in 1905 to a reporter for the *Compiler*, a local newspaper:

> ... on June 30, 1863, I got word to go out to Schrivers on the Mummasburg road, that a sick man there needed attention. I discovered the man to be a dropped Rebel, he couldn't march along and was left behind and had taken quarters in the Schriver barn . . . .

> I visited the man in the Schriver barn and prescribed for him. He was from New Orleans and was overmarched. He died later and was buried by the roadside.

Forty-two years later when speaking to the reporter, Dr. O'Neal probably did not remember the exact details, but his physician's visiting books, which he kept for each year of his practice, had the facts. On page 154 of the 1863 journal is this entry:

"Died on Mummasburg Road at Shrivers from 9th Regiment Louisiana, Hayes Bd, etc. J.W. Shackelfore, Rocky Mount, Bossier Parish. His mother [is] Mary A. Shackelfore, same address."

The David Schriver farm had at least 23 Confederate graves located on it, most of which were "unknown" and by 1873 all traces of Shackelfore's burial place were gone. Whether or not his mother ever received word of his death is not known.[67]

Lieutenant John Allan, Adjutant, 6th Virginia Cavalry

On July 3, 1863, near Fairfield, Pennsylvania, the 6th Virginia met the 6th United States Cavalry in a sharp skirmish which claimed the life of this officer. Major C.E. Flournay, the commander of the 6th, reported the event on July 18, saying:

"In this fight, my adjutant (Lieutenant John Allan) was killed while gallantly leading the regiment. In his death the service loses a gallant soldier and most efficient officer."

One of the men in the ranks of the 6th during that brief encounter was John N. Opie. In 1899 he wrote this:

110

At Fairfield, in the engagement with the regulars, we lost our adjutant, John Allan. In his pocket-book, was a note, written and dated the evening before, to this effect:

'Anyone who will deliver my body to Mr. _____, my father-in-law, No. _____ St., Baltimore, Md., will receive the sum of $500.'

We delivered his body, together with the note to a citizen, and afterwards learned that he carried out the request and received the money. This is one of the many instances I know of where men had a premonition of death.[68]

Private John Keels, 15th Alabama Infantry

During the July 2 fighting on the southeastern spur of Little Round Top, Colonel William C. Oates gave a graphic description of the wounding of one of the men in his regiment when the order to retreat was given.

> When the signal was given we ran like a herd of wild cattle, right through the line of [Union] dismounted cavalry-men. Some of the men as they ran through seized three of the cavalrymen by the collar and carried them out prisoners. As we ran, a man named Keils, of Company H, from Henry County, who was to my right and rear had his throat cut by a bullet, and he ran past me breathing at his throat and the blood spattering. His windpipe was entirely severed, but notwithstanding he crossed the mountain [Big Round Top] and died in the field hospital that night or the next morning.

Keel's gravesite did not survive. In fact, of the 1,200 or so identified Confederate burials in the Gettysburg area, only two are from the 15th Alabama, both listed at the Michael Fiscel farm, the Union Army's Fifth Corps hospital.[69]

Colonel William D. DeSaussure, 15th South Carolina Infantry

Born in Columbia, South Carolina, this officer was forty-four years old when he died from wounds received on July 2. He was called "The superior of [General] Kershaw's fine set of Colonels, having, from nature, those rare qualities that go to make up the successful war commander, being reticent, observant, far-seeing, quick, decided, of iron will, inspiring confidence in his leadership, cheerful, self-possessed, unaffected by danger, and delighting like a game cock in battle . . . . He exposed himself with reckless courage, but protected his men with untiring concern and skill."

DeSaussure had raised a company in 1846 and served through the Mexican War. He was married to a "Miss Ravenel" of Charleston.

Colonel DeSaussure had been mortally wounded while walking into battle, with sword in hand, at the front of his regiment somewhere just to the southwest of the famous "Wheatfield."

Augustus Dickert noted: "Just as we entered the woods the infantry opened upon us a withering fire, especially from up the gorge that ran in the direction of Round Top . . . . The Fifteenth Regiment met a heavy obstruction, a mock-orange hedge, and it was just after passing this obstacle that Colonel DeSaussure fell."

Carried to McLaws' Division hospital at Francis Bream's "Black Horse Tavern," he died there, and was buried in the center of the old McClellan burial ground just north of Bream's stone tavern. His body was removed after the war to his family plot in South Carolina. This is one of only a handful of gravesites which may be visited today with certainty.[70]

Sergeant Matthew Goodson, 52nd North Carolina Infantry

In Concord, North Carolina, stands a grave marker in the First Presbyterian Church's Memorial Garden. Surprisingly, however, there are no bones mouldering away under this granite stone. The body, that of Sergeant Goodson, still lies in an unknown, unmarked grave hundreds of miles northward at Evergreen Cemetery in Gettysburg, Pennsylvania. Goodson's story is this:

On July 3 during Longstreet's assault against the Federal line on Cemetery Ridge, Matthew Goodson was seriously wounded and captured. He was taken to the Jacob Schwartz farm southeast of town where he was cared for by Union doctors in the Second Corps hospital. His wound was through the lungs, the bullet coming out the left side, and caused his death on July 12. Goodson was then interred in the second row in one of the three hospital burial sites at this farm, in a cornfield called "Yard D."

In January of 1866 a local resident of Gettysburg, Hiram Warren, wrote to Goodson's wife, Catharon J. Young, and stated that he had discovered Sergeant Goodson's grave and was having it reburied in Evergreen Cemetery, where he personally would mark it well, care for it, and make sure it would never be lost.

Later that month the cemetery Board resolved that a portion of "Area E be set aside for the burial of the Rebel dead, beginning west of Ivy Rock and extending continuously westward and southwards as far as possible or may be necessary." On January 29, a grave was prepared in Lot #169, Section E for Matthew Goodson.

But unexpectedly, in August, 1867, the cemetery Board decided to "move the Rebel dead buried in Ever Green Cemetery to a more secluded place . . . ." This vote effectively eliminated Goodson from the earth, as his grave from then on was lost forever. Both in 1914 and in 1979 descendants of Goodson's family unsuccessfully attempted to locate this final resting place, and today the "secluded place" is still unidentified.[71]

Lieutenant James M. Seals, 42nd Mississippi Infantry

Emily Souder was one of the many volunteer nurses who worked so hard to relieve the suffering of many of the 21,000 wounded left behind at Gettysburg after the battle. And these nurses were, in fact, as kind to the Confederates as to their own men. On July 20, 1863, Ms. Souder wrote to her sister-in-law who lived in Philadelphia. In part, this missive reads:

> I wrote a letter yesterday for Lieutenant Seal, of the 42nd Missis-

sippi, a very interesting young man. On Wednesday morning last, we first visited the camp hospital of the Second Corps . . . . We had scarcely entered the field of labor when some one came and begged me to see a young Mississippi lieutenant . . . . Lying on the ground, in front of one of the large hospital tents, was a young man, whose face, as I looked at him, seemed that of one of my own kindred; the same blue eyes, brown hair, and light complexion. With sorrow, I spoke of his coming North *on the wrong side.* A Massachusetts man in the tent eagerly answered for him: "He could not help it; he is a good Union man at heart."

This was Lieutenant Seals. In reply to my offer of service, he said I could do nothing for him. He was groaning in spirit, and suffering greatly, having been wounded in five places, and had also suffered amputation . . . . Yesterday, I wrote his farewell message to his wife, which he was scarcely able to utter, even in a faint whisper.

Lieutenant Seals died shortly afterwards and was buried in Yard B, 2nd row located on a hill between the Jacob Schwartz and George Bushman farm houses. Unfortunately, by 1873 his grave was lost, and when 3,320 rebel remains were shipped South between 1871 and 1873, his bones were unidentified.[72]

Captain Samuel W. Gray, 57th North Carolina Infantry

When two of General Jubal Early's brigades attacked the Union line upon Cemetery Hill on the night of July 2, Captain Gray was one of the killed. Dr. J.W.C. O'Neal noted in his journal that he was buried at the east base of the hill just to the south of Raffensberger's Spring. The body was marked under the inspection of Captain C.H. Hawkins of the Eleventh Corps. O'Neal wrote:

. . . Locket on his breast . . . Capt. Gray is said to have been wounded in the head, and died at once - his memorandum book and a likeness was returned to his family. - Captain was 21 years of age - small man - in his uniform when killed. His father visited battle field Nov. 13, [1863] - making inquiries.

The father, from Winston, North Carolina, was able to find and remove his son's remains during his stay. The captain's body now rests in that beautiful state.[73]

Private Dawson W. Arnold, 5th Florida Infantry

Of the thousands of amputated limbs which were removed from wounded Confederates in the days and weeks following the battle, most ended up in their own unadorned burial places in numerous locations at field hospitals throughout the Gettysburg/Adams County area. Very likely most of these limbs have slowly decomposed in the deep holes where they remain today. Thirty years after the war Surgeon B.W. James visited the site of the Second Corps hospital where he had worked so hard in July 1863. James recalled:

113

I speedily ascertained the exact location; and the depression in the ground which we made for the blood and water [from the operating tables] to run into, was even visible, while some two or three little elevated, moundlike spots indicated the places where we buried the many limbs which we were obliged to remove.

Eventually, a number of these limbs of both Union and Confederate soldiers ended up as "specimens" at the Army Medical Museum, which was being established during the Civil War and was opened to the public in 1867. One of these specimens was the left femur of Private Dawson Arnold. The file on this individual bone states:

> Private W. [D.] A_____, G. 5th Florida, aged eighteen, was wounded July 3, 1863, at the battle of Gettysburg, by a conoidal musket ball, which shattered the upper third of the left femur. He was first treated in a field hospital, but on August 5, 1863, was admitted to Camp Letterman General Hospital. At that date, the patient was reduced by profuse suppuration; he was greatly emaciated, and large bed-sores had formed on his back. On August 12th, a troublesome diarrhea set in. He lingered till September 15, 1863, when he died from exhaustion. The large foliaceous masses of callus uniting the fragments are extremely delicate and brittle.

The specimen is number 1938 in the Surgical Section of the Museum. The overall event of Arnold's death is surely sad enough without the added insult of having one of his body parts turned into a museum exhibit.[74]

Colonel Henry K. Burgwyn, 26th North Carolina Infantry

This brave, young officer was mortally wounded on July 1 on or near Edward McPherson's farm northwest of Gettysburg in the severe fight against Meredith's "Iron Brigade" and the 150th Pennsylvania Infantry. Burgwyn was shot as he carried the colors of his regiment,

> with his sword in his hand and cheering on his men to victory - the ball passed through the lower part of both lungs and he lived about 2 hours - among his last words he asked how his men fought and said they never would disgrace him. He died in the arms of Lt. [Louis G.] Young bidding all farewell and sent love to his mother, father, sisters, and brothers.

The colonel was buried on July 2 by Young and another friend

> under a walnut tree about one mile west of the town on the north side of the turnpike road - 75 yds. N.E. of a medium sized stone farm house, which has a large yellow barn on the opposite side of the road. There are several graves under the tree but his is directly east of the tree with the head strait towards it.

Another officer, Captain Sam Mickey, recorded the place in his diary saying, ". . . I found Col. Burgwyn's grave under a tree, in a large field near a stone house, and Capt. [William] Wilson's and Capt. [William W.] McCreary's graves near by."

Lieutenant Louis Young wrote directly to Burgwyn's father reporting that, "I have buried him as well as possible under a walnut tree on the turnpike leading from [Gettysburg] to Chambersburg, 2 miles from the former place in a field about 100 yards from the road."

Burgwyn's corpse was encased in a crude wooden box and a friend, an artilleryman named W.E. Taylor, Jr., cut off a lock of the colonel's hair for his mother. In the spring of 1867 his remains were brought home from Gettysburg and reinterred in the Soldiers' Cemetery at Raleigh.

In 1868, Dr. J.W.C. O'Neal's journal indicated that the graves of Captains Wilson and McCreary were still visible on the property of Charles B. Polley about 1 3/4 miles northwest of the Gettysburg borough line and on the north side of the Chambersburg Pike. According to these several excellent directions, it would seem possible today to be able to travel to and stand on the exact spot where these sad but historic events took place so long ago. Lamentably, that is not as easy as it may seem. For one thing, Mr. Polley, in 1863 did not live in a stone house, but had recently built a new brick farmhouse. That structure does not appear to be standing in 1990. It is likely that the stone building mentioned by Burgwyn's friends stood nearby, and no longer exists.[75]

This shingle marks, as near as it is possible to determine, the site of Col. Burgwyn's 1863 grave. The Chambersburg Pike is in the distance.

Lieutenant Colonel John T. Ellis, 19th Virginia Infantry

It is not often that one reads of casualties that were suffered by Pickett's men *prior* to the charge made about 3 p.m. on July 3. It is known, however, that about 500 men were killed or disabled during the great 1½ to 2 hour bombardment preceding the assault. One of the unfortunate men to be spared that terrible march into history was John Ellis. In a reminiscence written in the 1890's, Lieutenant William N. Wood gave a clear eyewitness account of the colonel's death.

> The shells, bursting over and behind us, sent missiles upon anyone who might be lurking in the rear. Again the enemy was overshooting the mark and doing but little damage to the infantry. From Roundtop, two miles to our right, came those miserable enfilading solid shots which frequently struck the ground on our right, ricochetting along the line to the death and injury of many. Lieutenant Colonel John T. Ellis was lying in a small wash on the hillside, as one of these balls came bounding from the right. Some one hollowed - "look out" and he raised his head just in time to receive the ball in the face. Kind friends bore him to the shade, where death eased him of all pain. In Colonel Ellis we lost a good officer - a good man as well as a polished gentleman.

The 19th Virginia, alone, lost 20 killed and wounded just during the bombardment. Ellis was described in the official report of the battle as a man of bravery who with "his innocence, purity, and integrity as a Christian . . . endeared him to all who knew him."

John T. Ellis was born in 1827 in Amherst County, Virginia, and later attended Virginia Military Institute. He worked as a merchant at the outbreak of the war and was wounded in the thigh in 1862. His military records indicate that after receiving the horrible wound at Gettysburg he was taken to Pickett's Division hospital at the John F. Currens farm near Marsh Creek where he died on July 3.

Ellis was buried southeast of the house in an orchard under an apple tree. In August 1872, he was disinterred to Richmond and now lies in the famed Hollywood Cemetery of that city.[76]

Lieutenant John R. Presgraves, 8th Virginia Infantry

Clarissa F. Jones, a schoolteacher from Philadelphia, came to the battlefield shortly after July 3 to nurse the wounded. She did most of her good work for the battered members of Pickett's Division who ended up in the Union Second Corps hospital along Rock Creek.

Her first case was Lieutenant Presgraves whom she found on a rock being cared for by a brother. [John R. had three brothers, George, William, and James, all captured at Gettysburg.] Said she:

"The anxious brother did not even have a hankerchief; he was bathing the boy's wounds with a piece of paper."

Ms. Jones did everything in her power for John Presgraves. She learned from the brother that the four boys were from the James River area of Virginia and had a father who loved them all dearly, and who was more like a big brother to them all. John was cared for by the young fellow until he died four days later. Permission was granted for the lad to walk into Gettysburg in order to purchase a pine coffin. He especially wanted to do this he said, so that after the war someone could return and remove John's remains to their home in Virginia.

The next day nurse Jones and Jane Moore read the burial service over John's corpse, and it was tenderly laid to rest west of the Schwartz farmhouse in the woods on what was called "Red Hill."

The brother told Clarissa Jones that he would soon escape, which, as she related, he accomplished. Evidently the boy kept his promise, as John Presgraves' body was taken up sometime between 1865 and 1870 prior to the general disinterments of all Confederates to the South.[77]

Sergeant William S. Jinkins, 7th North Carolina Infantry

A great proportion of the men who made the attack under Pettigrew, Trimble, and Pickett on the last afternoon of the battle were killed or mortally wounded and died while still on the battlefield along Cemetery Ridge. Most of this number were buried indiscriminately in mass graves. One, in a sense, fortunate enough not to be among these was 34-year-old William Jinkins. His lonely grave was visible for several years after the battle in the orchard of Peter Frey who lived in a small stone house on the Taneytown Road. The orchard appears on contemporary maps to be just south of the farm buildings on the west side of that roadway. As in so many instances, by the early 1870s when Dr. Weaver began removing the Southern remains, the sergeant had become another "unknown" and had disappeared forever.

Jinkins' death, however, did not go unnoticed but was recorded by a Union soldier, Lieutenant Abner R. Small, who happened upon the scene the day after the assault had been repulsed.

> My duties permitting, I went among the wounded in a grove on the left of our position, where lay many hurt survivors of the rebel attacking force; men of Pickett's division, and Heth's, and Pender's. I proffered what assistance I could. I remember stopping beside one poor fellow who was shot through the body. His wants were few. 'Only a drink of water. I'm cold; so cold. Won't you cover me up?' Then his mind wandered, and he murmured something about his mother. Then he had a clear sense of his condition. Would I write to his home, and say how he loved them, and how he died? 'Tell them all about it, won't you? Father's name is Robert Jenkins. My name is Will.' I thought I heard him say that he belonged to the 7th North Carolina and came from Chatham County. His words faltered into silence. I covered his face.[78]

Private Samuel Parish, 28th Virginia Infantry

The story surrounding Sam Parish is one of the most interesting and somewhat most confusing of any yet researched. Robert Krick's *Gettysburg Death Roster* does not list him as one of the killed, but does note a "Samuel Parrish, 57th Virginia Infantry" as having died as a result of the battle. Kathy Harrison and John Busey in *Nothing But Glory* do not denote a Parrish in the 57th's roster, but do indicate a Samuel Parish, in Company E, 28th Virginia Infantry. He is reported to have enlisted in August of 1862 near Richmond and the company reports him wounded and subsequently as killed. And curiously, no Federal records are available on him in the National Archives. Who then was Sam Parish?

Ironically, two different and unrelated sources recall this young man and his death in the Union Second Corps hospital on the Jacob Schwartz farm. Here are excerpts from their detailed penned accounts concerning the elusive Sam Parish.

Jane Boswell Moore spent four weeks in the field hospital of the Second Corps. In her journal on or about July 10 she was asked by a citizen to visit the Rebel encampment which was, "on a gentle slope of ground directly back of our tent and beyond the hollow," and see a Rebel boy who was in a dying condition, and wanted someone to talk to about Jesus.

> I went at once, and in a shelter-tent on some straw, his gray blanket thrown aside lay a lad of nineteen, shot through the lungs, and breathing with great difficulty .... It was Samuel Parish, of the 28th (Rebel) Virginia Regiment .... Seating myself on a log in front of his tent, I began by making some inquiries as to his condition and history. He told me he had been in the army twelve months; that whilst away at Suffolk his mother had died, but he spoke of a young sister to whom some one had written. He had never been wounded before, and when I remarked, This will about end your battles .... he answered, Oh yes, I know that before to-morrow's sun rises I shall be gone ....

Moore continues her story by relating how she preached to him about Jesus, etc., and how he seemed at ease with his approaching death. Before she left, Parish requested that she draw his socks on his feet, as the fleas troubled him.

On the following day Moore noticed a group of nurses at his tent. "They told me he was dead, but I saw he was perfectly unconscious and dying, slowly struggling for breath, which he continued to do nearly all day."

J. Howard Wert relates the second story about young Parish. Wert, his father Adam, and mother Catherine, lived about one mile east of the Schwartz farm where Samuel lay dying. Catherine, or "Aunt Katy" as she was affectionately called, spent many hours at this hospital attending to the needs of some of the 3,000 wounded who suffered there. Wert wrote that, "above and beyond all others her love went out to a poor illiterate orphan boy - Sam Parish of Botetourt County, Virginia, one of the thousands who had fallen in Pickett's Charge." Wert recalled that Parish was a complete heathen or pagan in a Christian land.

The boy told Aunt Katy that his parents died when he was a baby and he could remember neither of them. An uncle took him in and he was constantly beaten, bruised, kicked, cuffed, and starved for many years. His only friend was an older sister, who lived with another relative. Parish had an ambrotype photograph of the sister, which he often showed to Catherine Wert. When the war came along, Sam was only sixteen. " . . . I was so glad when they agreed to take me. My uncle was very angry, but an officer threatened to arrest him for opposing the Southern cause . . . . In the army I had enough to eat most of the time and was treated like a man. I always tried to do my duty, but now this ends it all, and I only wish I could see my sister again."

Mrs. Wert tended Parish, and helped to reinforce his religious beliefs before he died. J. Howard recalled the burial and "his pain-drawn and wasted features. I saw his body wrapped in a blanket and placed with twenty others in one of the trenches that dotted the fields of the Schwartz farm, and, as men in blue hurriedly filled in the ground, mine were the only tears that fell for the orphan waif."

These reminiscences seem to verify that there was indeed a Private Samuel Parish who died at Gettysburg. His remains were never positively identified. Dr. J.W.C. O'Neal's journal lists a "Samuel Parrish, 57th Virginia" who was buried in Yard D - the cornfield, 1st row, and was disinterred to Richmond in the 1870s "with others" in one of 13 boxes marked "S."[79]

Colonel Hugh R. Miller, 42nd Mississippi Infantry

At 3:00 p.m. on July 3 near Seminary Ridge southwest of Gettysburg, General Joseph Davis's brigade formed in line of battle. The right regiment was the 42nd Mississippi commanded by Colonel Miller. Moments later the colonel was severely wounded in what would soon become known as Longstreet's assault, and oddly, in a report of the battle written in August, 1863, General Davis failed to mention anything concerning Miller's fate.

Hugh Reid Miller was born in 1812 in South Carolina but by the year 1840 he had become a full-fledged citizen of the state of Mississippi. Entering the service as a captain in '61 he became colonel of the 42nd on May 14, 1862.

Two people visited Colonel Miller when he lay seriously wounded at Gettysburg. The first, Andrew B. Cross of the U. S. Christian Commission, who, at the 3rd Division camp of the Union Second Corps hospital on July 8, recalled:

> In a fence corner just above us, among our men, lay Colonel Hugh R. Miller, of Pontotoc, Mississippi, . . . an eminent lawyer and judge of that State, shot through the left breast and right knee. We gave him a little wine and a cracker, which he took with great modesty, saying he was not dangerously wounded, but was thankful for our offer to write to his wife, Mrs. Susan G. Miller, at Sunnyside, Cumberland Co., Virginia.

The Surgeon told us his case was dangerous. Calling again after a short time to see if he would have anything, he modestly said: 'I am very much obliged to you, but give it to those around, who are worse, and need it more.' On the 20th we met his son in the office of Colonel [Henry C.] Alleman, stating that his father was dead, and requesting liberty to accompany his body home.

The second individual to remember Miller was Chaplain Thomas D. Witherspoon of the 42nd who had remained in Gettysburg for a few weeks after the battle to tend to the Confederate wounded. He said:

On the very day [July 19] before the order came to break up our field-hospital, tidings had come to us that the Colonel of the regiment in which I served, Colonel Hugh R. Miller, was lying mortally wounded at a private residence in Gettysburg, and had expressed a desire to see me. I reached his bedside just in time to receive his dying expression of his faith in Christ and his readiness to depart. Through the generosity of the kind family (a Maryland family) at whose home Colonel Miller had been so assiduously and tenderly cared for, the services of an embalmer were secured, and the body skillfully embalmed and inclosed in a metallic case. The Commandant of the Post at Gettysburg, whose name I do not recall, but who was a true gentleman as well as true soldier, on application being made to him to send the remains through the lines by flag of truce, did all he could to further this end. For he not only sent the remains to Baltimore in charge of one of the members of his staff, but he allowed Edwin Miller, the youthful son of the Colonel, and myself, his chaplain, to accompany the remains as escort with a letter to General [R.C.] Schenck, the Commandant at Baltimore, requesting that we should be permitted to accompany the remains by flag of truce to Richmond.

The scene on the arrival at General Schenck's headquarters in Baltimore was one that beggars description. The polite and gentlemanly Lieutenant who had accompanied us presented the letter from his superior officer, and it was handed to Colonel Fish, General Schenck's Adjutant. He read it, and asked, 'Where is the body?' The Lieutenant produced the receipt of the Adams Express Company, who had it in charge, and the Colonel, receiving it, handed it to one of his subordinates, and said, 'Go and get that body and have it buried.' 'Where shall I bury it?' asked the surprised official - to which the answer was in substance that he did not care where, so as the body was put out of the way, adding that he had stood all that he was going to stand of this paying honors to Rebel dead.

Edwin Miller, overwhelmed with the thought of the dishonor about to be done to his father's remains, plead most earnestly to be permitted to accompany the officer and see the remains interred, and it was only after a long interval, and through the intercession of friends of Colonel Fish, who were the witnesses of the boy's agony, that he was permitted to accompany the remains to their sepulture, and have them placed in a vault instead of being buried in the ground.

The lieutenant and Witherspoon were then thrown into a cell where they remained for some time.

The colonel's body eventually reached Richmond where a funeral was held at the First Presbyterian Church on July 29. On January 23, 1864, about five months later, his wife, Susan Gray Walton Miller, died and was buried alongside Colonel Miller, where they both rest to this day.

Interestingly, on July 4, 1863, an official correspondence crossed the battlelines at Gettysburg under a flag of truce. It was directed to General George G. Meade and was signed by General Robert E. Lee. This document is one, if not the only, communication which occurred between the commanders of both armies on that field. It asked Meade if, as a personal favor to himself (Lee), he might ascertain the condition of Colonel Hugh Miller. In all probability this must have been done, considering the situation which followed.[80]

Private Robert S. Phillips, 42nd Mississippi Infantry

An excellent letter survived which details the last days of Robert Phillips. It was written by Chaplain T.D. Witherspoon some five months after the battle to a brother of the deceased, Lieutenant J.W. Phillips.

> Dear Jim . . . It was my sad privilege to be with your brother through all his suffering from the time when he received his wound on the 3rd of July to the 14th the day of his death, and it will therefore be in my power to communicate something of interest to you. His wound was in the foot and at first was thought to be of a non-critical nature but it putrified, accompanied by feverness of the system, and a few days later after it was received inflammation set in, and it was found necessary to amputate. Your brother was at first very unwilling to have the limb amputated; but before the operation was performed became thoroughly convinced that it was indispensable . . . .
>
> So on the 9th of July the limb was skillfully removed. I had gone in person to Gettysburg for chloroform and superintended all the purchases. I did not see the operation performed but learned from several who saw it that it was a very successful operation. Your brother was well nursed by Mr. William Terry of his company . . . .
>
> I think I am justified in saying that his death was not caused either by his wound or by the amputation alone but by the wound in connection with an inflammatory state of the system which finally resulted in inflammation of the bowels and caused his death. I think it possible and I may say probable that if his leg had been amputated on the 4th or 5th he would have recovered, but it was impossible to foresee this and I think that the whole treatment of his case by the surgeons was skillful and proper . . . .
>
> Often when I gently chided him for taking too gloomy a view of his prospects for recovering he would look up and say, 'Do not misunderstand me I am not afraid to die.' 'I know in where I have put my faith.' Of his wife and family he would often speak in the most endearing

terms, expressing his longing to see them again . . . .

I was absent from the hospital . . . [for a] time and as soon as I came back hastened to see him. When I arrived he was speechless and in a short time afterwards sank gently and quietly into the arms of death. We buried him near our hospital by the side of Lieut. Geo. H. Howze and many others of our brave comrades who fell in that bloody struggle. His grave was marked and should the headboard be removed William Terry could no doubt identify the grave so as to secure the remains. It was sad to bury our brave men in that hostile land; but there was some comfort in the thought that they were sleeping upon the field of their glory . . . .

Unfortunately, although the whereabouts of Lieutenant Howze's grave was still known in 1866 [Samuel Lohr's farm] and was recorded by Dr. O'Neal, Phillips's burial place was not then chronicled, and unless moved by the family, it became another small pile of bones which ended up in a common grave somewhere other than Mississippi, or was left to decompose in an unforgiving Pennsylvania meadow.[81]

Private Edgar Hammond, 1st Maryland Battalion
An unidentified officer of a North Carolina regiment, possibly the 47th, who was wounded and ended up in the Confederate hospital at Pennsylvania College just north of Gettysburg, remembered the subject of this sketch. He wrote:

. . . it is strange how cold wounded men will get, even in the warmest weather. I saw one poor fellow on the field, named Hammond, from Anne Arundel County, Maryland, who was riddled with balls and slowly dying. He continually asked to be covered up, he was so cold, and I put my jacket over him though *I* too was shivering with cold, yet it was in July.

Three years later, while the officer was writing the story above, Dr. O'Neal recorded Hammond's barely marked grave located with one other Confederate in the cemetery at Mark's "White Church" on the Baltimore Pike, which had been a hospital of the Union's First Corps. But by 1870 it too, like so many others, had disappeared.[82]

Colonel Daniel H. Christie, 23rd North Carolina Infantry
Daniel Christie was born in Frederick County, Virginia, in 1833, but moved to North Carolina where he established a military academy several years before the war. Christie was wounded at both Seven Pines and Gaine's Mills in 1862. At Gettysburg he was again wounded fighting on the John S. Forney farm near Oak Ridge on July 1. After receiving his injury he remained for a time at the Forney house. Later in company with Lieutenant Colonel Johnston, and Major Blacknall, he made his way to the Jacob Hankey farmhouse a short distance up the Mummasburg Road. These men all stayed at Hankey's until the retreat began. The house had a well and

pump on the front porch and the water from it, little though it was, kept these wounded men alive and somewhat comfortable. During the stay at the Hankey farm Colonel Christie had the surviving handful of the 23rd North Carolina regiment brought to the door and "with much feeling assured them that he might never live to again lead them into battle but he would see that the 'imbecile [General] Iverson never should.' "

Christie was carried back on the long retreat to Virginia, where on July 17 he died in Winchester, and there he was buried.

The well and ancient pump where these men desperately fought to live, and where the dirty, ragged, battle scarred survivors of the 23rd listened to the impassioned speech of Colonel Christie are still visible today on the site where the old Hankey farmhouse once stood.[83]

Captain Jameson H. Moore, 11th Mississippi Infantry

A notation in Dr. John W.C. O'Neal's journal states that Captain Moore was "killed" on July 3 (probably mortally wounded during Pickett's Charge) and was buried on the Samuel Lohr farm, which was one of Hill's Third Corps hospitals along the Chambersburg Road.

Evidently, Moore's father attempted to locate his son's remains twenty years after the war. This letter to Dr. O'Neal from Dr. Weaver tells some of the story, and also gives the reader some pertinent information on Weaver's difficult tasks in exhuming the thousands of rebel gravesites at Gettysburg.

> On September 10th 1872 I shipped to the Ladie's Hollywood Mem. Assoc. of Richmond, Va. the remains of 683 Confederate Soldiers. It was J.H. Moore, Capt. Co. H, 11th Miss. regt. and 259 was the no. of the box which contained the same. I made six shipments in all to Richmond during the two years in which I was engaged in that part of the work, and the entire number exhumed and sent by me to R-d was 2965. With each shipment I sent a complete list or register explanatory of each box as to known or unknown, locality of exhumation. Hence, when Mr. Moore sought information at R-d, at once an examination of the lists in their possession would have shown that box 259 contained the remains of Capt. Moore &c-. However, I can understand all [my] lack of interest in such inquiries and, so can you, when I tell you that the Association yet owes me, for that great work, including interest over ($11,000) eleven thousand Dollars! You have had an extensive correspondence with the friends of the Confederate dead and I judge that, from your acquaintance with many prominent personages of the South, most probably you might be just the one to exercise a favorable consideration in behalf of my interest in the above debt . . . .
>
> I may drop a note to Mr. Moore stating that I had recd a letter of inquiry from you &c.

Captain Moore, initially, had been buried in Samuel Lohr's woods, on the north side, four miles up the Chambersburg Road with many others of his division.[84]

Major Robert H. Poore, 14th Virginia Infantry

On August 15, 1863, a notice appeared in a local newspaper, the *Star and Sentinel*. It read: "Major R.H. Poore of Fluvanna, fell about half way up the heights of Gettysburg, which his regiment was assisting to storm. He was first wounded in the hand, but refused to retire, though urged to do so by his officers. He continued to cheer his men and urge them forward, until he fell with one thigh badly fractured, and a flesh wound in the other. He was last heard from eleven days after the fight, at which time he was in a hospital near Gettysburg."

"Any of the returned surgeons or prisoners who may know any thing of his condition, will confer a great favor to his family by making it known."

A comrade stated that after being wounded Poore said that "so long as he could move to the front he should *advance*; that officers should give the example to their men; that the soldier's path of duty was *onward*."

The only word concerning the major's plight at Gettysburg was in Dr. O'Neal's journal where he noted:

"Removed to 12th Army Corps Hospital."

The family finally heard of his death, but no one ever found out where Poore was buried, or the final disposition of his body.[85]

Sergeant John Moseley, 4th Alabama Infantry

Last letters from soldiers mortally wounded in battle are quite rare. The few that have survived were usually written by friends, or nurses of the men as they lay dying and were often penned in the exact words of the soldier. An example of this practice is mentioned by Captain Azor Nickerson, who was seriously wounded on July 3. He says:

> The first volunteer attendant I saw on the field of Gettysburg was a woman: She carried writing materials, envelopes, and postage stamps, and wrote letters to the friends of those who were too desperately wounded to do so themselves. She took down just what each wanted to say, without abridgment, and in this manner many a mother, sister, and sweetheart received their first, last, and only message from their loved ones, whose lives ebbed out on this fatal field.

One such letter was from Sergeant Moseley.

Battlefield; Gettysburg, July 4, 1863

Dear Mother:

I am here a prisoner of war, and mortally wounded. I can live but a few hours, at farthest. I was shot fifty yards from the enemy's line. They have been exceedingly kind to me. I have no doubt as to the final result of this battle, and I hope I may live long enough to hear the shouts of victory before I die. I am very weak. Do not mourn my loss. I had hoped to have been spared; but a righteous God has ordered it otherwise, and I feel prepared to trust my ease in his hands. Farewell to you all! Pray that God may receive my soul. Your unfortunate son, John.[86]

Private Hardy Graves, 6th Alabama Infantry

Upon entering the Roman Catholic Church on July 2, Elizabeth Myers, a Gettysburg schoolteacher noticed three wounded Southern soldiers lying just inside the door. She recalled:

> I did what I could for them . . . One of them particularly attracted my attention. He was, or seemed to be, a large man though as he was lying down, I could not very well tell. His complection was dark, and he had the blackest eyes and hair I ever saw. That was fifty years ago, but today I can see him as distinctly as then, lying there helpless and the appealing look in his great black eyes.

Several weeks later while working at the general hospital on the York Pike, Elizabeth Myers had an occasion to go into the "dead tent" where several soldiers' corpses waited for burial. Myers continued:

> We went into the "dead tent" and there lay the man who had attracted my attention in the Catholic church, but the great black eyes were forever closed. On his breast was pinned his name - Hardy Graves; and below it his wife's name and address - Julia Graves, Brundidge, Pike County, Alabama. I cut off a lock of his hair and sometime after . . . I wrote to her, sent her the lock of hair, and told her what I knew of her husband. She replied, and asked me if I could find his grave . . . . He had been buried in a plot of ground along with many others, near Camp Letterman. I gathered some wild flowers growing near and enclosed them in a letter to her, telling her how her husband's grave was situated and that it was marked.

Private Graves, age 25, had been buried in Row 1, plot 18 in the Confederate section of that hospital graveyard. His death occurred on July 25. His was one of the remains which was still intact when removed to the South in the early 1870s. Hardy Graves had been wounded on July 1 when O'Neal's Brigade attacked Robinson's Division on Oak Ridge, northwest of Gettysburg.[87]

Private John E. Scammel, 1st Virginia Infantry

The entire experience of being in a field hospital was always a nightmare, but the first few days in the newly established Union Second Corps hospital near Rock Creek were horror almost beyond belief. A young Confederate officer, himself wounded, recalled those awful scenes, and specifically the pathetic death of one of his own company. Lieutenant John E. Dooley, in his diary on July 4 explains:

> The first man who attracted my attention upon being assigned to my position on this dreary hillside was one of the members of my company, John Scammel. Poor Scammel! He is standing up in his usually inert way, and wringing water from a blanket which he has been fortunate enough to preserve. There appears nothing very grievous in his condi-

tion, but he opens his shirt and quietly points to a piece of shell which is half buried in the hollow between his breasts. He tells me in a low complaining voice that he feels his time has come and that no one will by proper care give him a chance, if there be any chance, to recover from his wound. I bade him lie down and keep as quiet as possible and if I should meet with a surgeon that I would get him some attention.

Later:

> A young surgeon is near me now, and after examining my wounds and asking a great many foolish and ignorant questions, I urge him to look at the wound in my man's (Scammel's) breast. He assures me positively that he will do so as soon as he has taken a bite of something to eat. Oh humanity! A human life or a cup of coffee!

Then, the next day:

> July 5th. Morning dawns at last. Though raining still the chill of the small hours before day break no longer makes me shiver, and soon the carriers come around with their vessels of coffee, and this does much towards comforting the inner part of man. An officer (Yankee) is enquiring if any one here is acquainted with John Scammel. I tell him that he belongs to my company. "Here, then," he said, "are some little things I took from his pocket; he died a few minutes ago just a few yards off." These little effects consist of a five dollar Confederate bill stained with his blood, and a paper showing the date, etc. of his enrollment. Poor fellow, he might have lived if proper care had been shown him. But our poor fellows are dying all around us and but little surgical attention might save them.

The removal of Scammel's personal papers may have sealed his fate, as no record of his burial on the Schwartz farm has survived.[88]

Lieutenant Giles H. Cooper, 24th Virginia Infantry

Desperately wounded and crippled during the advance of Kemper's brigade on July 3 against the Union left center, Lieutenant Cooper must have spent a terrible night, unattended, and in severe pain lying somewhere along the Emmitsburg Road. Finally moved to the Union Second Corps hospital two miles in the rear on July 4, he endured his pain alone and unnoticed until discovered by Lieutenant John Dooley of the 1st Virginia, who said:

> About two yards from me on the other side of the road is a Virginia Lieut; 24th Va. His leg is torn and mangled fearfully; it is now amputated between the thigh and knee. There he reclines with his back against a stump and his wounded stump of a leg dragging heavily on the ground, clumsily bound up and portions of the flesh exposed and bedraggled in the mud. I have watched this officer pretty closely and although I have seen much pain and agony in his expression, I haven't heard a single word of complaint or impatient exclamation break from his lips.

Only once I heard him ask of some negro camp attendant in a tone of piteous expostulation to make a little fire near him, for the night was cold and the rain was chilling him to the very marrow of his bones. No fires were made however, for whether it was against orders or the result of neglect, we suffered a great deal from rain and the chilling night air. My poor friend appeared to suffer so much that after a selfish contest with my better impulses I sent him over my oil-cloth, that being doubled up and placed under his amputated member it might free him from much pain and distress. This gave him much relief and he appeared quite grateful; and now we were both equal in regard to exposure to the weather, for neither of us had any covering except our clothes. Long have I remembered this noble example of patience, and although I don't know what became of my Virginia friend, I have often recalled his quiet unexampled equanimity.

Cooper died on July 27 — he had hung on to life over three weeks. This officer was initially buried in Yard B of that large hospital, which was on a hill between the Jacob Schwartz and George Bushman farms. In 1872 his meager remains were shipped to Richmond in box #202, where they were interred in a common grave in Hollywood Cemetery.[89]

Colonel Lewis B. Williams Jr., 1st Virginia Infantry

This Virginia Military Institute graduate was born in 1833. He entered the service in 1861 as a captain of the 13th Virginia. Later he was promoted to lieutenant colonel in the 7th Virginia, then to colonel of the 1st in April, 1862. Williams was wounded and captured at Williamsburg and again at Gettysburg, where on July 3 he was one of sixteen officers of Pickett's Division who went into the attack mounted. Struck in the shoulder, he then fell from his horse onto his drawn sword, one eyewitness said. Lieutenant John Dooley next saw him just in rear of the Union line early on July 4.

This morning I am unable to walk a step and have myself carried about ten yards off the [Emmitsburg] road to where Col. Williams lies mortally wounded. Poor Williams . . . ! In the charge yesterday, foolishly and insanely he rode cooly and deliberately in front of the regiment . . . .

His spinal bone is broken, the shot, I think, striking at the neck joint and running down the spinal column. He suffers continual and intense agony. No position in which he may be placed affords any relief and he constantly seeks some change in the disposition of his head. There is a Yankee Col. close by who is doing all he can to alleviate the sufferings of those around him, and he most cheerfully offers to assist our Col. whenever he appears to suffer most. But Williams shows a dislike to be thus waited on, and frequently he asks me to give a more comfortable position to his head, which on account of the stiffness of my own wound, I am unable to do without giving him much additional pain. I make several of the officials who have direction of the ambulances promise me to have Col. removed to the field hospital where medical attendance may be had; and towards the middle of the day I have the satisfaction of knowing he had been removed. I never saw him afterwards. He died after 4 or 5 days' intense suffering.

As of this writing, Colonel Williams' "battlefield" burial place has not been determined. He may have been removed very soon after the war by his family.[90]

Colonel Lewis Williams, Jr. 1st Virginia Infantry (L.A. Wallace, Jr.)

Private Thomas W. Sligh, 3rd South Carolina Infantry

Private Sligh, approximately 18 years old when he joined the Confederate service, had been a college student at Newberry College, South Carolina. He was described as having fine qualities of head and heart — was a general favorite — witty, and kind. Sligh was said to be rather feminine in appearance and physically not very strong. By 1863, he was acting as orderly at regimental headquarters, and at Gettysburg his last moments were described by D.A. Dickert.

> Just before the Third Regiment went into action, . . . it became necessary . . . that the field and staff of the regiment should dismount . . . . On this occasion the Adjutant said to young Sligh:
> 'Now, Tom, get behind some hill and the moment we call you, bring up the horses; time is often of importance.'
> To the Adjutant's surprise Sligh burst into tears and besought that officer not to require him to stay behind, but on the contrary, to allow

128

him to join his company and go into battle. At first this was denied, but so persistent was he in his request that the Adjutant, who was very fond of him, said: 'Well, Tom, for this one time you may go, but don't ask it again.' Away he went with a smile instead of a tear. Poor fellow! The Orderly, Thomas W. Sligh, was killed in that battle while assisting to drive back General Sickles from the "Peach Orchard" on the 2d day of July, 1863.

Young Tom's body was not seen again, and his name does not appear on any post-war burial lists. He was apparently interred in one of the many unmarked graves on the George Rose farm.[91]

Colonel John B. Magruder, 57th Virginia Infantry

A twenty-four-year-old graduate of the University of Virginia, Colonel Magruder was born in Scottsville, Virginia. He entered the service as the captain of Company H, 57th Virginia.

Just as Magruder was crossing the stone wall on Cemetery Ridge with the remnant of Armistead's Brigade, he was hit by two musket balls both in the left chest and upper right arm, the bullets crossing in his chest. Seeing Cushing's rifled guns just in front of him, Colonel Magruder had just shouted, "They are ours!"

At the Second Corps field hospital, between July 4 and "a few days afterwards," Magruder was fortunate to be assisted by Catherine Wert, a local citizen who was mentioned in an earlier story. Her son, J. Howard Wert, wrote the following concerning the last hours of the dying colonel. Speaking to Mrs. Wert, Magruder said:

> I am sinking. I will never leave this Northern land alive. Some day, when peace is restored, my friends in old Virginia will carry my bones to the ancestral burying ground. But I will never more join the family or social circle. Death is creeping up on me. The surgeons are very kind and try to encourage me, but I feel my race is run. I have faced my duty as I saw it like a man, and I have no regrets . . . .
>
> But now, when the shadows of death are closing around me, I fear, madam, I may not have been as earnest in the discharge of religious duties as I should have been. I must soon face my maker. Madam, will you pray for me . . . ?

The Confederate colonel lingered a few days longer, and then he too passed away. But each day, until the final call of the stern messenger, Catherine Wert clasped his hand on her daily visits and knelt in prayer by his cot; and each day the colonel cheerfully said: "Madam, I thank you. I see a light beyond the darkness."

John Magruder did not have to wait until peace was established between North and South. After initially being buried in a cemetery at the Schwartz farm, his body was disinterred to Richmond in October, under a flag of truce. His remains and personal effects had been carefully placed in a metallic coffin by a fraternity brother of Epsilon Alpha.[92]

Captain William T. Magruder, Davis's Brigade, Heth's Division, Hill's Corps

When General Joseph R. Davis wrote the report of his brigade's actions on July 3, 1863 he noted that, "Capt. W.T. Magruder . . . [was] in action, and rendered valuable service." The reader may find it odd that Davis did not mention that Magruder, who was his assistant adjutant-general, had been killed or mortally wounded in that last attack on Meade's lines south of Gettysburg. His death surely occurred for this notice appeared in the local paper on July 30, 1863:

LOST

A large size double case watch and link chain belonging to Captain W.T. Magruder, C.S.A., who was killed at Gettysburg, July; and thought to have been placed in possession of Captain W.D. Nau, Co. B, 11th Miss. Regt., who died, July 13th, at 1st Army Corps, 2d Division Hospital, and who, it is supposed, gave it to someone previous to his death for safe keeping. The full value of the watch will be given for its return and the information gratefully received. Apply to: Mrs. Mary C. Magruder, 64 Courtland Street, Baltimore.

Magruder's name did not make it into any burial record of Confederates interred on the field or at U.S. hospitals. It is possible that Mrs. Magruder was able to secure his remains shortly after the battle.[93]

Lieutenant John A. Oates, 15th Alabama Infantry

William C. Oates, the brother of this subject, saw John Oates fall just after the captain of Company "G" was shot down in the attack on the south end of Little Round Top, July 2. He recalled the sad incident, saying " . . . my dear brother, succeeded to the command of the company, but was pierced through by a number of bullets, and fell mortally wounded." It is ironic that just prior to the fight John was very sick and was lying on the ground in rear of his company. William continued:

I thereupon told him not to go into the action, but when we advanced to remain where he was, because he was unable to bear the fatigue. He replied, with the most dogged and fiery determination, 'Brother, I will not do it. If I were to remain here people would say that I did it through cowardice; no, sir, I am an officer and will never disgrace the uniform I wear; I shall go through, unless I am killed, which I think is quite likely.'

These were the last words ever passed between us. When he fell, struck by several balls, Lieut. Isaac H. Parks, who had been his school-fellow, ran to him and dragged him behind a large stone, and just as Parks let him down another ball struck one of his hands and carried away his little finger.

Captured and carried to the Union's Fifth Corps field hospital at the Michael Fiscel farm, Lieutenant Oates lived 23 days. A companion, Lieutenant Barnett H. Cody, was with Oates at this hospital, where he died on July 23. Colonel William Oates explained:

> A Miss Lightner, a Virginia lady and Southern sympathizer, nursed them to the last, and Doctor Reed, of the One Hundred and Fifty-fifth Pennsylvania Regiment, did all that he could for them and had them decently buried when they died. He sent to me by flag of truce my brother's old gold watch, his pocketbook, and money. I endeavored for years after the war to find Doctor [J.E.A.] Reed without success, but finally obtained his address, Lancaster, Pennsylvania, and had a very pleasant and satisfactory correspondence with him. I had theretofore never had an opportunity of expressing to him the full measure of my gratitude for his attention to my brother and Lieutenant Cody.

The two young lieutenants were buried together east of Fiscel's house across a little creek. They were among twelve remains shipped south in the early 1870s. Only four names were still known in this small rebel cemetery, but none of the twelve could be identified separately.[94]

Private William P. Yearger, 22nd Georgia Infantry

This youthful infantryman was wounded late on July 2 when General A.R. Wright ineffectually made one of the last attacks that day against Cemetery Ridge. Yearger was evidently carried to the Union Second Corps hospital where he caught the attention of John Y. Foster, a civilian nurse from Philadelphia who was assisting the U.S. Christian Commission. Foster was in that hospital from July 10 through July 14 and said of Yearger:

> A soldier from Georgia was brought to our hospital greatly prostrated from the loss of his left leg. We at once saw that his case was hopeless, and bestowed upon him the closest care possible under the circumstances. From the first his mind seemed full of images of home, and he talked of little else besides his relatives. 'I have an old father at home,' he would say, 'and brothers and sisters; oh, if I could only go to them and sit in their midst once more!' Then his thoughts would seem to go back to the beginning of the war, and he would bemoan his folly in having entered the army, declaring, with despairing voice, that his heart had never been in the contest - that he would give years of his life if he could only go back again and be as he was before he took up arms.
>
> 'You can never know,' he said, 'what we have suffered in our army. We thought when we enlisted that the life of a soldier was full of charms - even those of us who volunteered purely in obedience to popular clamor and not from any principle, thought we should not after all be so very badly off; but we have all long ago found out our mistake.'

Mr. Foster soon had to inform William that he would die, and should now take time to dictate a letter to his family. This completely shocked the boy and he cried out with a great sob, "I am not prepared to go." Foster calmed him and, "after a while he roused himself and begged me to write what he should dictate."

131

Foster said:

> Then all the love in his heart poured forth. He told his father how he had suffered on the field; how he had been wounded and cared for by strangers and enemies; how he was dying with no hands but theirs to soothe and minister to him. Then he implored the father never to permit his younger brothers to go to the field, telling him they would but go to their death, and it would be in vain; victory could never be theirs. Then, when all else was said, he bade me write a word of farewell to each of the dear ones by name, concluding all with: 'Father, brothers, sisters, I hope to meet you in heaven' - a sob lying between each word as he gave them to me to write.

The following day William was much worse and at last his hour had struck.

> Half erect, leaning on my arms, he stretched out his own, spreading his palms heavenward, lifted his eyes with an inexpressible longing upward, as if he would appease, in one last absolute surrender, divine justice; and so, without a word, he died, his head falling on his breast, his hands dropping limp and prone, life going out as softly as a summer dream flits its wing over the sleep of a babe. Though dead the pressure of that hand lies still in my palm.
>
> I clipped a lock of hair, as he had requested, from his pallid temples, wrote upon it the day and hour of his decease, and sent it with his small effects, by an officer of his regiment, to the friends he was never again to see.

Although several 22nd Georgia soldiers were buried on the Schwartz farm, Yearger was not among the known remains there when surveyed in 1866 and 1870.[95]

Sergeant Samuel Reddick, 2nd North Carolina Cavalry

In the outskirts of Hanover, Pennsylvania, on June 30, 1863 a skirmish was fought between forces commanded by General Stuart and General Kilpatrick. One of the casualties of this minor engagement was Sergeant Reddick who was wounded through the breast near the Karl Forney farmhouse on the Westminster Road. Reddick had then moved into the yard and climbed up the steps to the porch where he lay for several hours. That evening when Mr. Forney returned to his house he found the sergeant and three wounded Union soldiers lying in the front room on the northwest side of the house.

Sam Reddick was struggling with death, and the family cared for him and the Federals with equal fervor. Before he died on July 1, Samuel removed from his pocket a copy of the New Testament and asked the sister of Mr. Forney to, "send it to my home. That address [on the flyleaf] will reach my sister. She gave me this book when I left home two years ago, and she asked me to keep it and bring it back again when the cruel war shall have ended.

The Karl Forney house where Sgt. Reddick spent his last hours.
(Hanover Chamber of Commerce)

It has ended now for me."

Miss Forney soon wrote to the family and learned that Reddick's father was a clergyman who asked that the grave be marked. A year later some friends or relatives came to Hanover and took up the body to be reinterred in the village graveyard in North Carolina. The location of the original burial site was about 100 yards southwest of Hanover near a red barn covered with slate, along a fence under a locust tree by the roadside. A convenience store now stands in place of Forney's house.[96]

Lieutenant Valentine W. Southall, 23rd Virginia Infantry

This officer died of wounds received in the fighting at or near Culp's Hill just southeast of Gettysburg, as a member of Steuart's Brigade of Ewell's Corps. About ten years ago the writer purchased a map at a local estate sale. The map is one of many that were often drawn to assist in remembering or to locate the gravesites of Confederate soldiers in the Gettysburg area. This particular map gives excellent directions to the burial spot of Lieutenant Southall. Currently the original is in the possession of Kent M. Brown.

Dr. O'Neal wrote the following letters to Southall's family in conjunction with the plans to find and ship home that officer's body:

Explanation & distance in stepped yds
Viewing location of Grave
from A to B 3 yds is stepped from post to head of grave
  A " C 2   "   " to side of "
  D " E 4½ corner post to foot of grave   Old barn Hospital
  F " J " { from a post on dividing
              { line to bottom of grave
  H " D 12 yds

Plan of position of J.W. Southall's Grave near Gettysburg

Fence

Brick Dwelling
large barn

Mrs Inciltas Farm

Fence

H

There are no other bodies
Fence   buried near

A
B
C
D
E
F

wild cherry tree

Fence

Woods   Frame house

3   Fence line

CENTRAL R. Road

Woods

2   Fence line

Hunterstown Road
is about 2 miles East of
Gettysburg

Fence

Fence

Gettysburg

Distance from Pike
1 to 2 = 415 stepped yds
3 to 4 = 175 " "   "

House

1   Fence

York Turnpike

N W S E

Map reproduced by DAN FUHRMAN

134

Gettysburg, Pa.
June 10, 1869

Mrs. Lucy H. Wood
Madam

Your letter enclosing draft of the neighborhood in which the remains of your brother lies buried has just been received.

The measurements will enable the remains to be recovered beyond a doubt and it will be unnecessary to have the ground dug over. The road your drafts describes is the road from the Turnpike to the Hunterstown road. *There is no doubt as regards the corner of the field in which the remains ly.* The remains can be expressed to you, *at very little cost,* as by this time they are but the principal bones and would be held in a small box - which when received be screwed to the bottom of a usual sized coffin & interred in usual form. The weight would be about 35 or 40 lbs ... This is merely a suggestion, prompted by experience, & does away with the necessity of extrodinary expense of travel, *coffin express freight* etc., etc. which Cost estimate $6 to $7.

Gettysburg, Pa.
Aug. 10, 1869

Mr. Jos. W. Southall
Sir,

Today I had exhumed and packed the remains of Lt. Southall. The wounded bone is wrapped in paper & packed [on] top of box which you

The board marks the approximate location where Lt. Southall was buried after the battle. Mrs. Weible's barn stood to the right of the telephone pole.

can examine. The box I send by Morson's Express. The expenses are,

For digging 1.50
For horse and wagon . . . 1.50
For Box 1.75
Postage & gates about 50
$\overline{\$5.25}$

which amount I shall require to be paid the express office when the box will be delivered.

For your kind courteous manner of correspondence please except thanks.

Very respectfully
J.W.C. O'Neal

What may be of interest to the reader are the average fees for the following services in the Gettysburg area in *1863*:
— price of embalming - $20.00
— price of case and coffin - $15.00
— cost of transportation of remains to soldiers' home - $30.00 (approximately)

Today, a visitor to the Gettysburg area should have no trouble proceeding to the exact site where Southall's body rested for over seven years. The area has changed very slightly over the last 127 years.[97]

Private Harden H. Williams, 9th Georgia Infantry

A small news article appeared in the May 15, 1878 edition of the *Star and Sentinel,* a Gettysburg newspaper. It noted:

> A daguerreotype of a soldier was found on the Gettysburg Battlefield by Mr. A.W. Flemming in 1863. In house cleaning the other day the picture fell from the case and on the inside was revealed in pencil the name "H.H.Williams." Should the owner or his friend desire the relic it will be cheerfully handed over.

Could the photograph have been that of the Georgian Williams? Unfortunately we shall never know. In checking through the various rosters, only one man of this name was killed at Gettysburg, which of course does not mean the soldier who dropped the photograph was *killed*. However, this incident was included because Williams may have lost the photograph at the time of his wounding or death, where it was later found by Mr. Flemming.[98]

Corporal William H. Poole, 9th Louisiana Infantry

Lieutenant Henry E. Handerson of the 9th Louisiana was at Gettysburg with his regiment which was posted on the southern edge of the borough on both sides of Baltimore Street. He wrote what follows many years later:

> My own company at this time was skirmishing in the outskirts of the town, and one of the men who happened to be present volunteered to guide me to my comrades. Accordingly, we proceeded towards the

136

southern edge of the town, and scurrying hastily across the main street, which was swept by the bullets of the enemy's skirmishers, made our way through gardens and enclosures to a large, frame house, into the back door of which we entered . . . .

. . . at each of the front windows a couple of men were occasionally exchanging shots with the enemy . . . . [Later] Passing through a gate leading to a garden, we scampered at full speed across an open space of about one hundred yards to the shelter of another house, still nearer the enemy, behind which I found half-a-dozen comrades skirmishing with a force of the enemy a short distance below.

Corporal Poole was evidently one of the sharpshooters mentioned by Handerson. He was stationed on the second floor in the brick house of Samuel McCreary and was killed by a bullet which passed through a table he was using as protection or as a prop for his weapon. This table is displayed today in the museum of the Gettysburg National Military Park Visitor Center. The caption in the display case reads:

. . . [Poole] entered the house, pushed the table to a doorway opened south and while kneeling behind the table and using it as a gun rest, was shot through the chest by a Union [sharpshooter] . . . . After the battle Mr. McCreary and a neighbor wrapped the body in a blanket, carried it to Long Lane . . . [and] buried it . . . . After the war Poole's parents came to Gettysburg, were directed to their son's grave and had the remains removed to Louisiana.[99]

Private Jeremiah S. Gage, 11th Mississippi Infantry

During the height of the July 3 cannonade preceding Pickett's Charge, a litter was carried into a Confederate aid station somewhere behind Seminary Ridge. Surgeon LeGrand J. Wilson, 42nd Mississippi, saw a head raise up and recognized Jerry Gage. The young soldier had been wounded by a piece of shell which struck the left side near the stomach, tearing away the tissues, a rib and the spleen and fractured the left forearm lacerating it terribly. Gage asked if the wound was mortal. When answered in the affirmative, he asked for paper and pen to write his mother. A portion of that letter, which he stained with his own blood read:

Gettysburg Penn.
July 3rd.

My dear Mother
This is the last you may ever hear from me. I have time to tell you that I died like a man. Bear my loss best you can. Remember that I am true to my country and my greatest regret at dying is that she is not free and that you and my sisters are robbed of my worth whatever that may be. I hope this will reach you and you must not regret that my body can not be obtained. It is a mere matter of form anyhow.

This is for my sisters too as I can not write more. Send my dying release to Miss Mary . . . you know who.

J.S. Gage

Co. A, 11th Miss.

Later, as he neared death, Gage said:

"Boys, come near me, it's growing dark. I can't see you. Come round me and take my hand."

His last words were:

"I want you to bury me . . . . I want to be buried like my comrades. But deep, boys, deep, so the beasts won't get me."

Jeremiah Gage, 11th Mississippi Infantry.
(J.W. Silver)

The bluff overlooking Willoughby's Run on the old Arnold/Horting farm where Gage and others were buried by their comrades.

Jeremiah Gage was buried near where he died. This location was on the George Arnold (tenant) farm along the Fairfield Road near Willoughby's Run, probably where the field aid station of Davis's Brigade was situated. During the battle this farm was occupied by John Horting. Several other 11th Mississippi men were interred under a walnut tree near the southeast corner of the garden, until removed to Richmond during the next decade. This old farm where Gage and other brave men died is a long lost memory, swallowed up by the pitiless tread of progress.[100]

Private James Iglehart, 1st Maryland Battalion

Lieutenant Randolph McKim, in his recollections of the Civil War written in 1910, could not forget the death of a man in Company A.

> As we were on the march to the field, on July 1st, the distant booming of the cannon in our ears, one of the privates of Murray's company came up to me, during a brief halt by the roadside, and said he wanted to speak to me. It was James Iglehart, of Annapolis. We stepped aside, and I said, 'What is it, Iglehart?' He answered, 'Lieutenant, I want to ask your pardon.' 'My pardon!' said I. 'Why, what on earth do you mean?' 'I've done you an injustice,' he said, 'and before we go into this battle, I want to tell you so, and have your forgiveness.' I told him I could not imagine what he meant, and he then said that he had thought from my bearing toward him that I was 'proud and stuck up,' because I was an officer and he only a private in the ranks, but now he saw that he was entirely mistaken and he wanted to wipe out the unspoken injustice he had done me.
>
> The next time I heard his voice was in that last terrible charge on Culp's Hill, when our column had been dashed back like a wave breaking in spray against a rock. 'McKim,' he cried, 'McKim, for God's sake, help me!' I turned and saw him prostrate on the ground, shot through both thighs. I went back a few yards, and putting my arm round him, dragged him to the shelter of a great rock and laid him down to die.
>
> There are two things that rise in my thought when I think of this incident. One is that if he hadn't come to me two days before and relieved his mind as he did, the gallant fellow would not have asked my help. And the other is that the men in blue in that breastwork must have been touched with pity when they saw me trying to help poor Iglehart. It took some minutes to go back and get him behind that rock, and they could have shot us both down with perfect ease if they had chosen to do it.

Iglehart's grave was no more than a small space in one of the many Confederate burial trenches which dotted the ridges and fields near Culp's Hill and Rock Creek. Some of these trenches (and there may have been as many as seventeen) held fifty to one hundred corpses, and by the time they were disinterred, James Iglehart's bones had now become mingled with those of many other unknown Southerners along with the Pennsylvania soil which had so long blanketed those mournful hollows.[101]

Lieutenant George A. Howze, 42nd Mississippi Infantry

George Howze entered the service in 1862, two years after his marriage to Mollie White of Murfreesboro, Tennessee. When the war began he and his wife and infant son were living in Memphis.

On July 1, Howze was shot while his regiment engaged the enemy some time around eleven o'clock, on that bleak day. His black servant, Stephen, came out on the battlefield, searched for and found Howze's body, and carried it back to a field hospital near Marsh Creek. Stephen made a rude coffin for the lieutenant who was soon buried on Samuel Lohr's farm next to Robert S. Phillips of the same regiment. Both graves were well marked, but by 1870 only Howze's headboard was still visible when these remains went to Richmond, under the direction of Dr. Rufus Weaver. An eyewitness to Lieutenant Howze's last moments, Captain Robert W. Locke, who was himself struck in the side by a piece of shell, wrote:

> Lt. Howze, who was an amiable gentleman, came up & desired to know if I was hurt & said to me to 'take care of myself,' & raised up and started off. The Regt. was then falling back, he had gone but a few steps when he fell dead. His health was too feeble to have been in the field, but it was his first fight & he was a man of great pride of character & was determined to do nothing that might tarnish his honorable reputation.[102]

Lieutenant Joe C. Smith, 4th Texas Infantry

John C. West of Company E wrote this description of the final minutes of Lieutenant Smith as the regiment moved across the difficult terrain from the Michael Bushman farm toward the Devil's Den and Little Round Top areas.

> We went in pretty fair order across the field. As we entered the timber and brush our line was more broken. We soon struck a stone fence; then came a branch. Lieutenant Joe Smith, Company E, wet his handkerchief, wrung it out and tied it around his head as he moved up the slope, which we had now reached. Bullets and grapeshot were coming thick and fast. A bullet passed through his head; examination afterwards showed 11 holes through the folded handkerchief. I think it made a white mark for a sharpshooter.

If Smith ever had a grave, or if it was marked, his name never showed up on O'Neal's, Weaver's, or Frey's lists, and he was not an identifiable person in 1870 when many Confederates' remains were moved to Richmond, Raleigh, Charleston, or Savannah. Lieutenant Smith was more likely simply covered with an inch or two of soil, or a few rocks, or dumped into a crevice between some large boulders on Houck's Ridge, where the flesh and bones quickly rotted to dust under so many years of nature's merciless pounding.[103]

Private William Mitchel, 1st Virginia Infantry

This young soldier was another killed during Longstreet's assault on July 3. Some time after the war, Jane Mitchel, mother of William wrote to her surviving son, James, concerning the burial of his brother.

> [Charles Joice said that] after the battle he and three others were going on the field looking for wounded soldiers. And that they found Willie rolled in a blanket pinned with three pins. The center one being a large one with a black head and two others common pins — that his face had been washed and there was a slip of paper pinned to the blanket with his name 'W.J. Mitchel' son of the Irish patriot — with the help of a colored man they dug a grave on the banks of a small cabin* so close that no plow would ever disturb it — and laid him there and took the paper and fastened it to a piece of cracked board and hammered it there at the head of the grave. It was near a little brick house [N. Codori farm] that the body was found . . . .
>
> I would like to find that grave. It was years before I gave up the hope that he would some day appear. I got it into my head that he had been taken prisoner and carried off a long distance but that he would make his way back one day — this I knew was very silly of me but the hope was there nevertheless . . . .[104]

Major Benjamin W. Leigh, Johnson's Division, Ewell's Corps

At Gettysburg, Major Leigh was assistant adjutant-general under General Edward Johnson. Johnson said of him: ". . . (his) conscientious discharge of duty, superior attainments, and noble bearing made him invaluable to me, [he] was killed within a short distance of the enemy's line."

Lieutenant R.H. McKim who remembered seeing Leigh during the battle, said he found out years later from a Federal officer how that soldier died.

> It seems that Major Leigh, seeing a group of Confederates in a very exposed position [near the Union breastworks on Culp's Hill] raise a white flag in order to surrender to the enemy, gallantly rode into their midst to prevent the execution of their purpose. While so engaged he met his death, . . . the day after the battle he was found lying on the field *still in the saddle*, his horse dead with him as if a part of him - horse and rider having been killed at the same moment.

This incident occurred about 11 a.m. on July 3 in front of U.S. General George Greene's line. Later, Greene, impressed with Leigh's bravery, had the major buried within the Union lines near where he fell.

His grave was one of the only ones actually named and marked on S.G. Elliott's map which has been spoken about several times in this book. The

---

*"Banks" in this case may mean "foundation of a small cabin."

141

Major B.W. Leigh, who will rest forever in the National Cemetery at Gettysburg. (Museum of the Confederacy)

site was approximately 1/8 to 1/4 mile east-northeast of Philip Pfeifer's house on the Baltimore Pike, at the edge of a small Federal burial ground behind the earthworks. When this group of Northern dead was transferred to the new Soldiers' National Cemetery, he, mistakenly, was taken up and interred in a Yankee grave as "B.W. Laigh." The only personal item found on the corpse was $10 in Confederate currency. Today, Major Leigh still rests in the Unknown Plot of the national cemetery at Gettysburg.[105]

Captain James H. Burns, 6th North Carolina Infantry

Captain Burns was one of at least 47 men killed or mortally wounded in the 6th North Carolina regiment during the Battle of Gettysburg. He was probably wounded in the attack on Cemetery Hill on the evening of July 2. Carried back to the Elizabeth Weible farm, which was a field hospital for Hays' and Avery's (Hoke's) brigades, he soon died.

About seventeen months after the war ended, Burns' brother wrote to Dr. J.W.C. O'Neal in Gettysburg asking for assistance in recovering James' body. Here is one of the letters O'Neal wrote back:

142

Gettysburg, Pa.
October 5th, 1866

Mr. C.B. Burns
My dear Sir

The remains of your brother was sent to the express office yesterday. I saw them disinterred the day before - I found a grave (marked with his name) *alone*, back of the barn on the Walter [Weible] place, the front teeth as you described Sound. The clothing was so decayed that I could not recognize them. The buttons were not brass guilt as you described but military. The neck tie being silk was not fully rotted. So also a small military flag which I suppose he had pocketed as a trophy as also his shoulder straps all of which I have - & they are *subject to your order*. I have not at present the liesure to prepare pack & send them to you. The box was so rotted that the remains & ground was one mass. The marked board that stood at the head of his grave is in the box & whoever marked it will be able to recognize it - trusting I have satisfactorily attended to the trust. I have the pleasure of being very

Respectfully yours,
J.W.C. O'Neal[106]

Colonel Joseph Wasden, 22nd Georgia Infantry

At about five o'clock in the afternoon of July 2, General Ambrose Wright's brigade was ordered to advance toward the Union positions along Cemetery Ridge. Just as his brigade reached the half-way point, Wright said he lost Colonel Wasden, ". . . who was killed at the head of his command near the Emmitsburg turnpike. The service contained no better or truer officer, and his death, while deeply deplored by his friends and associates, will be a serious loss to the Confederacy."

The reader may remember that the site of Wasden's grave was enumerated in Part I. Colonel Horatio Rogers, 2nd Rhode Island, was one of the first men to view Wasden's body. On July 4 his regiment was on the picket line, and Rogers said:

Many dead lay on the Emmitsburg Road in front of us, and just opposite the right of the regiment, stretched at full length, was the lifeless form of a Confederate Colonel. His was a fine manly figure and he was smitten down in the prime of life. It was ascertained from a Masonic Certificate in his pocket that his name was Joseph Wasden, and that he was a member of Franklin Lodge, No. 11, of Warrenton, Georgia. Thereupon it was determined that this deceased brother, an enemy in life, that had been stricken down far from home and loved ones, should be buried by fraternal hands, and the Blue uniforms gathered round the gray, as a squad of the Second Rhode Island under the direction of Captain Thomas Foy, raised the inanimate form in their arms and bore it carefully two or three hundred yards to the right, where they tenderly and reverently buried it on the south side of Codori's Barn, the opposing picket shots serving as minute guns.

143

Corporal Archie Stalker prepared a marker out of the top of an ammunition box and carved the colonel's name, etc., upon it and erected it at the head of the grave.

Dr. R.B. Weaver subsequently wrote to Dr. J.W.C. O'Neal concerning the removal of Wasden's remains.

844 North 10th St., Phila.,
Oct. 27, 1886.

Dear Doctor:

It affords me pleasure to gratify your desire for information concerning the exhumation and reburial of the remains of Colonel J. Wasden, 22nd Ga. Regt., who was killed at Gettysburg July, 1863. During the summer of 1872 per contract with the Savannah Memorial Association, I exhumed the remains of Col. Wasden, and those one hundred Georgians who were buried on the Battlefield of Gettysburg, and shipped the same to the S. M. Ass'n, by whom they were reinterred in the Cemetery at Savannah, Ga. The grave, on the headboard of which was conspicuously marked 'Col. J. Wasden, 22nd Ga. Reg.' was located on the East side of the Emmitsburg Road, just inside the fence and was near the South end of Codori's Barn. The grave was single and alone. I exhumed the remains of Col. W. and packed them in a large box, No. 5, in company with those of eight other Georgians, whose names were known as their graves had been marked. The remains were not packed separately in small boxes, but collectively in large boxes by direction from the Savannah Memorial Association to meet the limited capacity

The site of Colonel Wasden's much visited grave just south of Codori's barn.

of the Soldiers Lot in the Cemetery. Any further information which may be desired concerning these remains can be received by addressing Mrs. John Williamson, President of the S.M.A., Savannah, Ga. I am fraternally yours R.B. Weaver[107]

Colonel David R.E. Winn, 4th Georgia Infantry

David Winn was born in 1831. Married to Francis M. Dean, he was working as a physician prior to the war, but in 1861 was commissioned as an infantry lieutenant in Co. K. Winn was killed early in the first day's engagement and was buried under a tree behind the barn and near the house of David Blocher. Adjoining Winn was another grave, that of Private Josiah Law of Company B, 4th Georgia, Dole's Brigade. These graves remained well marked for a number of years, apparently cared for by Blocher and his son, Oliver.

Colonel David Winn, 4th Georgia, killed on July 1. The Blocher's made it hard for him to rest in peace. (R.K. Krick)

The present day approximate location of Col. Winn's gravesite behind Blocher's barn.

Shortly after the war, Dr. Rufus Weaver's father, Samuel, attempted to remove Winn's remains and express them to the family in Georgia. Samuel Weaver was told by David Blocher that the family of David Winn would have to pay a fee to him in order to exhume the body. The family declined to pay, and the grave remained closed until October 1871 when Rufus Weaver removed these two bodies to the South along with the rest of the known Confederate deceased. When the body arrived in Georgia, Colonel Winn's gold plate and teeth had been removed from the skull, and Weaver had to eventually pay $5.00 to Blocher to have the plate returned.

Colonel Winn and Private Law's graves were two of just a few burial sites noted on Elliott's map, and Winn's is one of the most accessible of these old Confederate gravesites in 1990.[108]

Brigadier General William Barksdale, McLaws' Division, Longstreet's Corps

One of the most interesting stories of a Confederate general *to be killed or wounded* at Gettysburg was that of William Barksdale who was mortally wounded in the July 2 attack on General Daniel Sickles' "Peach Orchard salient" along the Emmitsburg Road. A private of the 114th Pennsylvania, William M. Boggs, said that he saw Barksdale's wounded body on the battlefield. In 1882 he drew a map representing where the general fell.

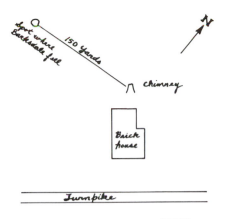

Map reproduced by DAN FUHRMAN

General William Barksdale.

Boggs reported:

"I had gone out in advance of our line to an old chimney that stood in rear of the brick house (Sherfy's I think was the name). With one other companion our attention was directed to a general officer leading the first line to the attack and we distinctly saw him fall."

Among the first Federals to discover this officer was Lieutenant Homer Baldwin, 5th U.S. Artillery who noted: " . . . Gen. Barksdale of Mis. was wounded in front of our battery on the 2nd. I gave him brandy and water that I got off a surgeon and fixed him up as comfortably as possible."

Barksdale was left on the field until dark when Lieutenant George G. Benedict, 12th Vermont, was told by a rebel soldier that the general was wounded between the lines and had begged to be brought in.

Benedict stated that four men of the 14th Vermont (one was Private David Parker) finally found him in the early morning of the 3rd.

A surgeon of the 148th Pennsylvania, Alfred T. Hamilton, attended Barksdale during July 3rd at the Jacob Hummelbaugh farmhouse, describing him as,

> large, corpulent, refined in appearance, bold, and his general physical and mental make up indicated firmness, endurance, vigor, quick perception . . . . He was dressed in the jeans of their choice.
> His short roundabout was trimmed on the sleeves with gold braid. The Mississippi button, with a star in the center, closed it. The collar had three stars on each side next [to] the chin. Next [to] his body was a fine linen or cotton shirt which was closed by three studs bearing Masonic emblems. His pants had two stripes of gold braid, half an inch broad, down each leg.

Barksdale died that same day and was apparently laid out in the yard of Hummelbaugh's house where he was seen again by Lieutenant Benedict later that day:

147

Hummelbaugh's yard, where Barksdale died and was buried.

> I saw his body soon after the life had left it . . . his vest thrown open disclosed a ball hole through the breast, and his legs were bandaged and bloody from gunshots through both of them. He had fought without the wig which Speaker Grow once knocked off in the Hall of Representatives, and his bald head and broad face, with open unblinking eyes, lay uncovered in the sunshine. There he lay alone, without a comrade to brush the flies from his corpse.

According to Private Henry Meyer, 148th Pennsylvania, the general was buried "in front of the house." However another source reported that he was interred "near the Hummelbaugh's house, . . . under a cherry tree south of the lane."

On a stake at the head of his grave was fastened the top of a "cardboard" box bearing a penciled inscription:

> Brigadier General Barksdale of Mississippi McLaws' division, Longstreet's Corps Died on the morning of 3rd July, 1863 Eight years a representative in United States Congress. Shot through the left breast, and left leg broken below the knee.

Some time afterwards Dr. J.W.C. O'Neal noted in his handbook that "Parsons Owens* has taken Barksdale's body to South Carolina." His body finally reached his home and is now interred in Greenwood Cemetery, Jackson, Mississippi.[109]

---

*Reverend W.B. Owen, Chaplain, 17th Mississippi Infantry

Private John Wesley Culp, 2nd Virginia Infantry

"Wes" Culp, a Gettysburg native was believed to have been born about 1839. His father was Jesse E. Culp, and he had two sisters, Anne and Julia, and a brother, William E. Some time prior to the war, Culp, who was employed as a carriage or wagon builder, moved to Shepherdstown, Virginia, when the owner of the small business, William Hoffman, transferred his operation to that area. In the late 1850s Wes joined a local militia company which, in 1861, became Company B of the 2nd Virginia Infantry. When other Pennsylvanians working for Hoffman were leaving for the North, Culp chose to stay in Virginia, where, in Harpers Ferry on April 20, 1861, he officially enlisted in the Confederate Army.

On July 2, 1863, while in the vicinity of his hometown as part of a hostile and invading army, John Wesley asked for permission to visit his family. Culp's friend, Benjamin S. Pendleton, an orderly to General James A. Walker, the Stonewall Brigade commander, arranged for Culp to meet the

John Wesley Culp who came home to die. (GNMP)

general who quickly authorized the leave. Pendleton also related that General Walker was happy to have a Pennsylvanian in his ranks. Culp soon called on both sisters. Julia was staying at a first cousin's house (William Stallsmith on York Street) and Anne Culp, who had married another local resident, J. Jefferson Myers, was at home on High Street.

Private Culp evidently participated in both the July 2 Thursday evening attack and the July 3 morning fighting on Culp's Hill. Ben Pendleton who saw Julia Culp on the evening of July 3 delivered the melancholy news that Wesley had been shot in the head and killed on July 3 and was buried "where he fell." The body was said to be "under a crooked tree" and Pendleton told Julia he had carefully marked the grave. When Julia went out to the hill, which was named after Henry Culp, a relative of Wesley's, she was unable to locate the site. The only item found was a broken musket buttstock marked "W. Culp." A former officer in the 2nd Virginia, H.K. Douglas, wrote:

"There also fell in that assault [July 3] Wesley Culp .... He was twenty-four years old and very little, if any, over five feet, and when captain of the company I procured a special gun for him .... He was buried there [on Culp's Hill] and sleeps there now."

Another Confederate who knew J.W. Culp was John Casler who stated in a memoir that "Billy" or Wes Culp was indeed killed on Culp's Hill on the third day of the battle.

John Wesley Culp's grave was never found. Was he actually buried by his comrades in a single grave, or was he one of the hundreds who were piled into indiscriminate gaping trenches where fifty to one hundred men were clumped together like cord wood, forever to remain an "unknown?"

Or was he in fact mortally wounded and carried with the injured to Maryland or Virginia, where he died days or weeks later and was buried somewhere in his adopted state? For now, these questions remain unanswered.[110]

Private William E. Hutchinson, 52nd North Carolina

The name associated with this particular biography is listed as one of the casualties of Pettigrew's Brigade, and turns up in an 1864 report published by the State of New York, pertaining to the relief of wounded and sick soldiers after the Battle of Gettysburg. One of the committees assisting Union and Confederate wounded in a Federal field hospital reported:

> As soon as possible, after our arrival, we devoted our time to the hospitals of the Union soldiers; on our way to one of them, a young boy who was trying to follow some Confederate troops, came towards us and laid down at our feet fainting in his exhaustion; when revived by wine, Mr. Barclay's kind manners won his confidence, and he begged to be 'taken home to his mother' who lived near Raleigh, North Carolina. In his pocket was a letter from her saying she should become crazy if she did not hear from him; the little fellow was fed and taken into a house

and placed in a comfortable bed and well nursed, but at the end of three days, without having had a wound, he died from exhaustion. His name was Wm. Hutchinson. His letters and a statement of his death and place of burial, were sent to his mother.

Hutchinson's burial, if marked at all, did not survive time nor the elements.

Private Patrick McNeil, Parker's Virginia Battery

On the morning of July 3, during an exchange of artillery with U.S. batteries, Private McNeil, a driver normally posted in the rear with the limber and caisson teams, was brought up onto the line to spell one of the exhausted gunners. An historian for the battery transcribed this scene:

> In the midst of the flying shells, Pat went out in front of the guns to bring to safety a wounded Federal who had been overlooked in the earlier rescue efforts. McNeil rolled the crippled enemy soldier onto his own back and then crawled back to the Confederate lines to relative safety for both of them. As he was finishing his errand of mercy, or perhaps just after it was accomplished, a cannon ball tore off both of McNeil's legs. The dying man gasped, 'Oh, my poor wife and children!' and lapsed into unconsciousness. A short time later he died at a field hospital.

This hospital was located along Willoughby's Run. Later, on July 4, several battery members dug a single grave for McNeil and another deceased comrade, Corporal James B. Loughridge, and they were buried as decently as possible under the circumstances. The names of these men were "cut into a crude pine board," after which the gravediggers returned to the work of caring for the wounded. No record of the disposition of this "twin grave" exists today.[112]

Privates Moore and Shelton, Regiments Unknown

This final biography is unusual due to the inordinate elusiveness of the subjects and their respective units. They have been included because of the minor action in which they died plus the relatively long distance from the Gettysburg battlefield where the two men were interred. Furthermore, they are an example of the numerous Confederates who may not have died on the famous battlefield but who nevertheless met their deaths as a result of the Gettysburg Campaign. Moore's and Shelton's lives ended in this way.

During the days just prior to the great battle at Gettysburg, units and detachments of the Confederate Army of Northern Virginia were moving throughout many parts of southern Pennsylvania in search of commissary stores or military weapons, equipment, and supplies.

Much of this activity centered west, southwest and northwest of Chambersburg, in the regions of Mercersburg, Ft. Loudon, and McConnellsburg. In the latter place, a small skirmish took place late on June 29 or early on June 30. The units involved were Company A, 1st New York Cavalry under

Captain Abram Jones plus a small militia force, and elements of Captain Irvine's (or Irwin's) company from rebel General John Imboden's command. The Confederate forces numbered about 63 and the U.S. troops 38, not including the uniformed militia, which was commanded by a "Captain" Dr. Winthode and had no more than 50 members present.

This insignificant engagement occurred as the Confederate unit entered the village of 700 or so inhabitants from the east, and ran into Jones's men (who were on a scout) who were resting in front of the Fulton Hotel. The Southerners, immediately retreated, and rode through a scattering fire from the Federals. The rebels lost two wounded, 32 captured and two killed.

A witness to this quick action remembered:

> I had run out to the east end of town and sat on the fence as the troops passed me, and as soon as they disappeared up the Mercersburg pike, I followed and saw a wounded rebel lying in the middle of the road, who was living. I got him to the side of the road. He was shot in the back between the shoulders and the ball could be seen just beneath the skin in his breast. He lived about fifteen minutes and gave me his name which was Wm. Shelton of Bath, Morgan County, Virginia. He said his wife's name was Mary. I wrote to her but got no reply. About one hundred yards east of this man lay another rebel but he was dead when I got to him.

The other man was named W.B. Moore, and was reported to be from Virginia. Shelton, in several different versions of the story was also said to have been from North Carolina. His initials and name were given as "William," "F.A." and "T.A." The bodies were buried by the local citizens "just inside of Daniel Fore's meadow alongside of the Mercersburg pike." For years the graves went unmarked. Finally, a citizen of the county, T. Elliott Patterson, Esq., erected a wooden marker at the site (a mile or so from the hotel by the side of the road) which read:

"Confederate Graves, June 30, 1863"

It is known that before the interment, both men were carried to the courthouse and lay there until coffins could be procured.

Another account of the affair says that, "One of the [32] prisoners still having his pistol shot his captor in the leg and Captain Jones, enraged at the act, cut the Rebel over the neck with his sword, almost severing his head from his body."

This severely wounded Confederate was taken along with the other prisoners toward Bloody Run (Everett) when Captain Jones moved out of McConnellsburg. This man died soon thereafter and was buried by the roadside.

The identities of these three Southerners have yet to be positively identified.[113][114]

Gettysburg — where so many poured out the wine of life; where the very name of the field brings tears to the eyes of thousands of mourners - is it any wonder that, with feet standing upon the sacred sod, the very air seems haunted, as well as hollowed, and every wind the sigh of a ghostly presence.

Sophronia E. Bucklin
Volunteer Nurse at Gettysburg

The lonely grave of an unknown Confederate soldier in the village cemetery at Mt. Holly Springs, Pennsylvania, 24 miles north of Gettysburg. He is one of many who died in out of the way places during the great campaign.

Appendix A
Marking the Grave

Oh! God preserve his remains for his Friends.[115]

Both armies, north and south, *had* regulations imposing strict rules as to how deceased soldiers were to be buried. Obviously these governmental procedures were not often followed on battlefields of the Civil War. In one case, however, these formalities were adhered to, to the letter. Surgeon John H. Brinton wrote this after visiting Gettysburg.

> In [a] churchyard, [the Trinity German Reformed Church] at one corner of the church building, I observed a number of new made graves, arranged with the greatest precision, each one of them being provided with a head board and foot board, made of shingles, the former bearing the name, rank, company and regiment of the man beneath. The head boards were exactly alike, the line for the inscription and the styles for the lettering being alike in all cases. . . . The Army Regulations had been scrupulously complied with.[116]

Sadly, many Confederates were simply not even buried at Gettysburg, and hundreds were just barely interred. Thousands ended up as "unknowns" in huge trenches, but approximately 1,200 were fortunate enough to have an individual gravesite and some type of identification placed upon it. Various ways were noted by eyewitnesses as to how these graves were marked. Here are a few examples:

1. The bark of a tree hewed off — name written in pencil or red chalk.

2. A board or shingle nailed to a tree over or near the grave.

3. A shingle or a piece of wood taken from an ammunition box, or "cracker" box placed at head of grave, with name carved or written in.

4. A piece of rail fence or post stuck into grave with name written in pencil or on a piece of paper attached.

5. A pile of stones placed over the grave, with name scratched onto piece of shale or slate.

6. The name chiseled into nearby rock or boulder.

7. Engraved brass or silver plate or plaque actually attached to grave marker.

8. A cartridge box flap nailed to a post with name carved into the leather.

9. Floor boards torn out of barn or house inscribed with soldier's name, regiment, etc.

Appendix B

Identifying the Corpse

It was heart-sickening to think of the deep agony which those few dreadful days spread abroad among the little groups at the firesides of fond homes all over the land. In fancy I saw the long procession of widows, and orphans, and kindred, who mourned for the slaughtered heroes.[117]

Sophronia E. Bucklin
Volunteer nurse at Gettysburg

The process by which Confederate corpses or remains were identified was interesting and at times morbid. Even those Southerners who were fortunate enough to have some type of identification placed on their burial sites, often, in more than 60% of the cases, that identification proved incorrect. Leander Warren, whose father was one of the first to engage in the business of disinterring corpses, wrote:

"A great number of the bodies were found with limbs or other body parts missing. A lot of the bodies were only skeletons while others still had decomposed flesh attached to the bones. Most were unrecognizable."[118]

The uniform, or remains of a uniform, could be a factor in correct initial identification. Personal possessions the soldier carried in his pocket or haversack, such as letters, diaries, a name scratched on a tin cup or canteen, for example, could aid the burial parties who accomplished the primary interment. If friends or comrades were present, obviously this was in the best possible interest of the deceased. "Dog tags" or "identification discs" were not much of a factor in Civil War burials as most Confederates did not own them since they were not issued, and they were almost impossible to purchase in the South.

When the demand for the return of Southern remains began, even as early as 1863, it was imperative, especially to the deceased soldier's family, that identification of the corpse or remains, be precise. There were several ways this could occur. The first, and best way was for the actual family member to travel to the battlefield or its environs, and locate the *marked* grave, exhume the bones or body and make positive personal identification. One deceased soldier's father at the Second Corps hospital found his son's body when he saw a certain pair of ivory shirt studs in the grave. A mother, after exhuming 15-20 old burials, finally recognized her son by a particular dented button which remained on his uniform blouse.

Ofttimes, after years had passed, it became necessary to describe the size and height of a former soldier, what he was wearing at the time of death, and most importantly what was the death wound and where on the body it was made. By that time headboards or other identification may have disappeared, and to men like J.G. Frey, Samuel and Rufus Weaver, Sam Herbst, or Dr. John O'Neal, these *fine points* of the body profile could make the difference between carrying home your true son, father or brother, or a

Captain George Rust Bedinger, 33rd Virginia, whose remains were never found. (L. Reidenbaugh)

misidentified corpse. For instance, in an 1865 letter to Mrs. C.B. Bedinger, who was searching for the body of her son killed at Gettysburg, Samuel Weaver said:

> Kind Madam,
> This noon I rec'd yours dated 25th inst. and in reply I am truely sorry that I cant give you the information you so much desire. I found but few [marked] Confederate graves on either the right or left or center where the heavy charges was made. . . . I can't find the name of Capt. Geo. R. Bedinger.
> If you could find out the location where he fell and likely where he was buryed and if you knew where he was wounded in particular if any of his limbs was broken or wounded in his head & if so which side of the limb right or left or which side of the head right or left or back or front, or something peculiar about the teeth [as] those bones and teeth don't decay. It may be that he had some tooth pluged that you can recollect which one it was and what side of the jaw and wether it was in the upper or lower jaw bone. . . .

It is apparent, that many graves were opened time and time again, and it is no wonder that so many quickly lost their identities.

Appendix C
Confederates Identified on Elliott's Map

In Part I, the burial map surveyed and drawn by civil engineer S.G. Elliott of F. Bourquin and Company, Philadelphia, was discussed. This map which reported to show the grave locations of thousands of Union and Confederate soldiers and dead horses, was probably completed some time before 1865. Of all of the burials noted on this map, only about 14 are identified. The answer as to why Elliott chose only these men as well as several Union graves to identify, is not known at this time. The Confederates listed on his map are indicated below.

Lt. Col. David R.E. Winn, 4th Georgia

Pvt. Josiah H. Law, 4th Georgia

"E.T. Covey," 4th Georgia (I.D. not correct)

Lt. R.W. Meacham, 13th Georgia

Pvt. James M. Williams, 6th North Carolina

Corp. William R. Butler, 4th Georgia

Lt. Hardy V. Gibson, 13th Alabama

Maj. Benjamin W. Leigh, A.A.G., to Gen. E. Johnson

Lt. W.R. Oursler, 17th Mississippi

Col. Joseph Wasden, 22nd Georgia

Appendix D

Confederates Interred in the National Cemetery

One [rebel], who lay mortally wounded in front of the 69th Pennsylvania, sullenly refused to be taken to the hospital. He said he wanted to die on the field where he fell.[119]

> Lt. Benjamin H. Child
> Battery H, 1st Rhode Island
> Light Artillery

. . . I here most conscientiously assert, that I firmly believe that there has not been a single mistake made in the removal of the soldiers to the cemetery by taking the body of a rebel for a Union soldier.

> Samuel Weaver

As can be expected, some Confederate corpses inadvertently were buried in the Soldiers' National Cemetery which was established shortly after the battle to hold and honor the Union dead killed or mortally wounded in the Battle of Gettysburg. Author John W. Busey first discovered the fact that a few Confederates were actually buried in that cemetery. During the last few years, Busey and Roy E. Frampton have added to this list. The following is an up-to-date roster of possible Southerners interred among the Federal dead at Gettysburg.[120]

Current Grave Identification	*Possible True Identity*
S. Carter Co. A 15th Conn.	Lieut. Sidney Carter, Co. A, 14th S.C.
Williams Co. D 20th Conn.	Cpl. David Williams, Co. D, 20th N.C.
M.F. Knott, 1st Md.	Ninon F. Knott, 1st Maryland, C.S.A.
S. Hindeman 15th Mass.	N.B. Hindeman, Co. A, 13th Miss.
J.L. Johnson Co. K 11th Mass.	John L. Johnson, Co. K, 11th Miss.
John Aker	James Akers, 2nd Miss.
J. Graves, Co. C 1st Pa.	Sergt. Thomas J. Graves, Co. I, 21st Ga.
E.T. Green 14th Pa.	Eli T. Green, Co. E, 14th Va.
G. Williams Co. A	Gresham G. Williams, Co. A, 3rd Ga.

"B.W. Laigh"
    Unknown Plot
	Major Benjamin W. Leigh,
	    Adj. Gen. on Gen. Edward Johnson's
	    staff.

Appendix E

Post-War Discovery of Graves

. . . all of the killed and mortally wounded were left in Pennsylvania, and no one knows their graves, if buried. It may be that some of their bones may have been gathered into . . . Richmond, since the war. Who knows? Others, doubtless, have whitened and mingled into dust on the field where they fell, which now the plow-boy, whistling as he plows, turns over as common earth, unconscious that his plowshare is stirring sod hallowed by the blood of as brave men as the continent has ever known.[121]

Captain Richard Irby
18th Virginia Infantry

Throughout the last 127 years, but especially from 1873 to 1930, farmers, workmen, and others sometimes accidentally stumbled upon the remains of Confederate and Union soldiers who had died and were buried in the Gettysburg area. Here are a few examples of those macabre discoveries.[122]

Gettysburg *Compiler*

October 11, 1877
Confederate Dead. In plowing, the other day, the bones of four Confederates were discovered a short distance east of the Springs Hotel. It is Gen. Slayton's intention to have them taken up and placed in some suitable spot on the Springs park, and have other remains of Confederates known to be on the battlefield removed to the same spot.

August 2, 1878
One day last week, Mr. Henry M. Mingay, commander of the GAR Post at Pen Yan, NY, found among the bones of a Confederate soldier buried near Blocher's shop, one mile north of this place, a daguerreotype of a lady and two girls 7 to 10 years old, in a remarkable state of preservation. The case had decayed, but the picture is still perfect, showing features, clothing, coloring and gilding with the clearness of recent taking. Mr. Blocher says the soldier belonged to the 31st Georgia regiment [Gordon's Brigade], and Mr. Mingay intends to have the facts well published, with a view to the restoration of the picture to the family of the deceased. . . .

June 9, 1881
Last week, as Mr. W.H. Gelback was having some plowing done on his place, near the Emmitsburg road, the bones of about twenty men were found, and he believes more are on the premises. He had them placed in a corner of the field, From the clothing remaining it is supposed the bodies belonged to the Confederate side. [today's Colt Park]

June 22, 1881
Mr. J.A. Danner . . . has a pearl medallion with turquoise set in gold in the center, marked "S.L.P.". It was found in the trench containing the bodies recently discovered on the Gelback place.

June 8, 1886
D.A. Riley, residing on the Codori Farm on June 5, plowed up the remains of a soldier in the field over which Pickett charged and near the [Col. G.H.] Ward monument. He showed us a piece of the skull with a bullet protruding at both sides, also one of the thigh bones with a bullet imbedded in its lower end. A cap box full of caps was also found. From indications the remains were probably one of Pickett's men.

August 10, 1886
Paul Kappes has shown us part of a human jaw bone, lower right side, filled with solid teeth, belonging to a much-decayed skeleton found in Menchey's sand hole, near East Cemetery Hill, last week. The body was no doubt that of a Confederate, the buttons and bullets found with the bones indicating that, and a bottle of ink, soundly corked, and bearing a Richmond label, corroborating it.

May 10, 1887

SEVEN BODIES FOUND — On Tuesday, in plowing, Mr. Frederick Peffer came upon the remains of seven soldiers, supposed Mississippians, near the 12th New Jersey monument, on the south side of Emmitsburg road. The bones were reburied.

Star and Sentinel

October 6, 1885

One day last week a son of Mr. Joseph J. Smith found a human skull embedded in the lot of the Water Company, on East Cemetery Hill. A small portion projected above the earth, and being curious the boy dug it out, with the above result. The poor fellow may have been buried there in July 1863 and been resting in an unknown grave ever since.

Note: This skull belonged to the Louisiana Confederate found by Caldwell on April 2, 1910.

May 29, 1888

Clayton Hoke, of Cumberland Township, shows us an interesting relic found by his wife on the farm of Hon. Edward McPherson, formerly owned by John S. Crawford, Esq., deceased. It is part of a decayed wooden head-board which bears in neat letters the following inscription: 'Capt. J.M. Gaston. Capt. T.C. Clark* & Son. 42d Miss. Vols. Killed July 1, 1863.' This farm was a vast rebel hospital.

* Captain Thomas Goode Clark, Co. I, 42nd Mississippi and his two sons were killed on July 1 (Jonathan and A. Henry)

July, 17, 1888

On last Thursday Jacob Mumper discovered and unearthed the remains of a soldier near the Devil's Den. Mr. Mumper was showing the beauty of the den to a tourist and when walking over the pathway, north of it, annually frequented by thousands of visitors, he discovered a human bone protruding from the ground. He immediately procured some digging irons and commenced an investigation, and, after going down about a foot, found the skeleton in good condition of a large man. All the bones were there but those of the right arm. In the superficial grave were found two or three Alabama buttons, some US buttons, a light gold ring, engraved in diamond-shaped form. Nothing found conclusively indicated to which army the soldier belonged. As the den was occupied by Confederate sharpshooters, the probability is that he was one of them, and the theory is corroborated by the finding of the Southern buttons. On the other hand the engraving of the ring might indicate that he belonged to our army, as the diamond was the Third Corps badge. No vestige of his uniform remained.

July 17, 1888

Yesterday Edward Leeper, while gathering herbs in Reynolds grove, discovered the remains of two Union soldiers. The buttons and remnants of uniform were conclusive evidence that they belonged to the Union Army. Further investigation will be made this morning. We have not learned what disposition was made of the bodies, but they will undoubtedly be reinterred in the National Cemetery with the 979 unknown comrades who sleep there.

July 21, 1888

Mr. William Heagy* informs us that several soldiers are buried in the woods on his farm. Whether Union or Confederate he does not know. Presumably the latter as the remains of the former were carefully collected shortly after the battle.

*Wm. Heagy farm was probably on South Cavalry Field.

July 23, 1888

Investigation shows that the remains of soldiers found by Edward Leeper, last week, were those of Confederates who had been removed & buried there several years ago.

December 11, 1888

Last week H. Speece, in digging a drain in Phillip Hennig's field, west of Seminary Ridge, uncovered the remains of a soldier. A few bones, pieces of blanket, a part of a leather belt, and several brass buttons, having on them the letter "I" were found in the grave.

July 22, 1890

The remains of a Confederate soldier were unearthed while workmen were digging sand at the Sand bank on the old Brick yard lane, east of Cemetery Hill. Buttons indicated he was a rebel.

November 18, 1890

On November 12 Charles E. Lady was crossing the field about 300 yds. Southeast of the Springs hotel. He came to where a dog had been digging in the ground. He noticed some bones & on closer inspection discovered a trench in which there were several skeletons, which are supposed to be those of rebels. Several buttons were found but they were too much rusted to tell from what state they were. An investigation will likely be made & should it be decided that the bodies are those of Union men, they will likely be buried in the National Cemetery.

Other Sources

Baltimore *Gazette*

CONFEDERATE DEAD — Gen. Bradley T. Johnson, D. Ridgeley

Howard and Lamar Hollyday, the committee appointed by the general committee of the Society of the Army and Navy of the Confederate States in Maryland to visit Gettysburg and provide for the proper interment of the remains of Southern soldiers found on the place of Mr. W.H. Gelack, will perform the duty in a day or two. They will box the remains up, bring them here and bury them at Loudon Park Cemetery, unless they are claimed by the survivors of Thomas' brigade of Georgians, to which the deceased soldiers are supposed to have belonged. [Baltimore *Gazette*] Party arrived at Gettysburg on 21 June 1881.

Adams County News

April 2, 1910

While cleaning up the premises of the Gettysburg Water Company on East Cemetery Hill Robert Caldwell, superintendent of the company, uncovered the remains of a human body, doubtless that of one of the "Louisiana Tigers" who participated in the charge on the Hill on July 2, 1863.

All of the body had become disintegrated with the exception of the bones of the lower limbs and some smaller bones of the body. The skull was entirely gone. With the body were found a table knife and spoon and the frame of a purse in which was an Indian arrowhead. There were no coins in the purse at all, evidently having been removed when the body was buried, if any were there at the time.

The charge on East Cemetery Hill was made by Hoke's North Carolina Brigade and by Hays' Louisiana Brigade, generally known as the "Louisiana Tigers." After the battle the bodies of the dead Confederate soldiers found on the slope of the Hill were buried, to be taken up later and buried in Southern cemeteries. Some of those buried on the slope of the hill were evidently missed as they were found at intervals afterward. Prior to the find of Mr. Caldwell the last was made about twenty years ago by Prof. Louis Sowers.

Prof. Sowers was waking one evening in the vicinity of Menchey's sand quarry when he noticed a shoe sticking out of the ground. Investigation showed a bone inside and further investigation disclosed the remainder of the body.

The bones found by Mr. Caldwell were located in the thicket along "Lovers' Lane" and are doubtless those of one of the men killed in the charge, buried there after the battle and missed when the bodies were disinterred to be taken South.

The bones were re-buried and the place marked by Mr. Caldwell to await instructions.

Letter dated April 23, 1934 to Arthur K. Willoughby from the

Superintendent of the Gettysburg National Military Park:

Late last summer there occurred one of the most severe storms ever witnessed in this vicinity. . . .

In checking damage to the Klingel farm along the Emmitsburg road, Mr. Blubaugh, (the farmer) discovered that a deep gulley had been cut out of his bean patch. Close examination revealed human bones and a little excavating unearthed the remains of the two Confederate soldiers, bullets, etc. . . .

Judging from the place of burial these soldiers were of Wilcox's "Alabama" brigade of Anderson's Division for it was on this terrain that these gallant soldiers turned "Sickles" right flank on the evening of July 2nd. . . .

The remains (were) placed in a box in the Park office and the Daughters of the Confederacy of Alabama were notified of the find, requesting advice as to the final disposition of these remains. It was finally decided to inter the remains of these heroes in the Confederate Cemetery in Hagerstown.

The bones of a Confederate soldier washed up on the D. Klingle farm in 1934. (GNMP)

Several years ago Earl J. Coates of Columbia, Maryland gave the author some interesting information concerning post-war discoveries of grave sites on the old Peter Baker farm which still stands on the north side of the Baltimore Pike just across the bridge over Rock Creek.

In 1964 Coates had spoken to the older of the Baker brothers who lived on the farm and was then in his early 80s. The old man had related how in the 1890s or about 1900 he remembered a search made on their property for Civil War graves. Baker said that the men brought along an elderly black man who would place his ear to the ground and use a large wooden mallet to "sound" for unusual hollow spots in the earth behind the barn. Evidently this man had a particular proficiency for locating these burial sites. So it seems that for a long time after the battle soldiers' remains were still being found in the Gettysburg area.

In fact, this writer knows of a Confederate soldier found in 1977 in the Union Second Corps' hospital along Rock Creek (1st position). The man evidently died soon after arriving at that field hospital as he was buried in his uniform jacket in an area soon vacated by that medical establishment. An old photograph of those remains are included here. As noted in Part I there may still be as many as one thousand graves or more undiscovered in the county.

The skeleton of a Southern soldier recovered on the Jacob Schwartz farm in 1977.

169

The grave of Pvt. Jules Freret, 2nd. Co. Washington Artillery (La) C.S.A. at Mount St. Mary's College in Emmitsburg, Maryland. Freret, who died of wounds received at Gettysburg, had attended this college before the war.

James P. Norton, Co. C, 8th Alabama was wounded in the leg on July 2. Five months later he died in a U.S. hospital in York, Pennsylvania. Norton had attended Mount St. Mary's prior to the war and is now interred there next to Pvt. Freret.

NOTES

1. J. Howard Wert, "In the Hospitals of Gettysburg." Vol. I, Harrisburg *Telegraph*, 1907.
Henry C. Morhous, *Reminiscences of the 123rd Regiment, N.Y.S.V.*, Peoples Journal Book and Job Office, Greenwich, NY, 1879.
"L.L.H." Letter printed in the July 16, 1863 issue of *The Lutheran and Missionary*, Philadelphia, Pennsylvania, August, 1863.

2. Sophronia E. Bucklin, *In Hospital and Camp:* ... J.E. Potter and Company, Philadelphia, Pennsylvania, 1869, p. 189.
Andrew B. Cross, *Battle of Gettysburg and The Christian Commission*, Philadelphia, Pennsylvania, 1865.

3. The casualty figures for Confederate dead vary according to the source. Thomas Livermore estimates 3,900; Robert Krick states that the old returns of Lee's army reflect 2,603 killed. His new estimates are 4,546 killed and mortally wounded. Kathy Harrison at the Gettysburg National Military Park estimates 4,500 to 5,000 killed and mortally wounded, which is probably as close as we shall ever come to the true count in this generation.

4. *The War of the Rebellion: A Compilation of the Official Records of the Union and Confederate Armies* (Washington, D.C., 1880-1901), Ser. I, Vol. 27, Part 1, pp. 119-120.
Ibid., pt. 1, p. 79.

5. Benjamin W. Thompson, *Personal Narrative of Experiences in the Civil War, 1861-1865*, Manuscript written in 1910 now in possession of J.A. Thompson, Minneapolis, Minnesota. Thompson was a captain in Co. F, 111th New York Infantry.

6. Henry R. Berkeley, *Four Years in the Confederate Artillery*. University of North Carolina Press, Chapel Hill, 1961. Berkeley, a private, served in the Amherst (Virginia) Artillery.

7. Robert Stiles, *Four Years under Marse Robert*. Morningside Press, Dayton, Ohio, 1977, p. 219.

8. Charles S. Wainwright, *A Diary of Battle*. Ed. by Allan Nevins. Harcourt, Brace & World, Inc., New York, 1962, p. 254.

9. Robert G. Carter, *Four Brothers in Blue*. University of Texas Press, Austin, Texas, 1979, p. 325.

10. Horatio D. Chapman, unpublished diary in the Connecticut State Library, Hartford, Connecticut. Chapman was a member of the 20th Connecticut Infantry.

11. Wyman S. White, unpublished copy of a diary in the possession of S.W. White, Fitzwilliam, New Hampshire.

12. Horatio D. Chapman, op. cit.

13. Daniel A. Skelly, *A Boy's Experience During the Battle of Gettysburg.* Gettysburg, Pennsylvania, 1932.

14. Clifton Johnson, *Battleground Adventures.* Houghton Mifflin Company, Boston & New York, 1915, pp. 195-96.

15. James Houghton, unpublished journal in the archives of the University of Michigan, Ann Arbor, Michigan.

16. Edwin Forbes, personal letter on file at the Pierpont Morgan Library, New York, New York.

17. Leonard M. Gardner, *Sunset Memories.* Gettysburg Times Publishing Company, 1941, p. 72.

18. J. Howard Wert, *A Complete Hand-book of the Monuments and Indications.* . . . R.M. Surgeon & Co., Harrisburg, Pennsylvania, 1886, p. 201.

19. Wyman S. White, op. cit.

20. Frank A. Haskell, *The Battle of Gettysburg.* Ed. by Bruce Catton. Houghton Mifflin Company, Boston & New York, 1957, p. 137.

21. Daniel A. Skelly, op. cit.

22. George G. Benedict, *Army Life in Virginia.* Free Press Association, Burlington, 1905, pp. 190-1.

23. John D. Bloodgood, *Personal Reminiscences of the War.* Hurt & Easton, New York, 1893, p. 149.

24. Albertus McCreary, *Gettysburg: A Boy's Experience of the Battle*, manuscript in the Adams County Historical Society, p. 17.

25. Jacob Hoke, *Reminiscences of the War.* . . . M.A. Foltz, publisher, Chambersburg, Pennsylvania, 1884, p. 172.

26. John D. Smith, *The History of the Nineteenth Regiment of Maine Volunteer Infantry*, 1862-1865. Great Western Printing Co., Minneapolis, Minnesota, 1909, p. 98.

27. Charles S. Wainwright, op. cit., p. 254.

28. J. Howard Wert, *In the Hospitals of Gettysburg*, op. cit., Vol. X.

29. Clifton Johnson, op. cit., p. 174.

30. D. Augustus Dickert, *History of Kershaw's Brigade.* Morningside Press, Dayton, Ohio, 1973, p. 249.

31. William C. Oates, *The War Between the Union and the Confederacy.* Morningside Press, Dayton, Ohio, 1974, p. 678.

32. Andrew B. Cross, op. cit., p. 26.

33. Frank A. Haskell, op. cit., p. 149.

34. J. Howard Wert, *A Complete Handbook.* . . . op. cit., p. 201.

35. Albertus McCreary, op. cit., p. 18.

36. *History of Cumberland and Adams Counties.* Warner, Beers Co., Chicago, 1866, p. 246

37. Kathleen Georg Harrison, *Confederate Burials at Gettysburg, a Compilation.* Gettysburg National Military Park Library.
Gregory A. Coco, *A Vast Sea of Misery. A History and Guide to the Union and Confederate Field Hospitals at Gettysburg.* Thomas Publications, Gettysburg, Pennsylvania, 1988.

38. Frederic S. Klein, (Ed.) *Just South of Gettysburg.* The Newman Press, Westminster, Maryland, 1863, p. 107.
Gregory A. Coco, *On the Bloodstained Field II.* Thomas Publications, Gettysburg, Pennsylvania, 1989, p. 20.
W.C. Storrick, *The Battle of Gettysburg.* McFarland Company, Harrisburg, Pennsylvania, 1975, p. 33.

39. Daniel G. Brinton, "From Chancellorsville to Gettysburg, A Doctor's Diary." The Pennsylvania Magazine of History and Biography, Vol. 89, 1965, p. 314.
A.K. McClure, "Old Time Notes of Pennsylvania." Philadelphia, Pennsylvania, 1905, p. 105.

40. Clifton Johnson, op. cit., p. 174. The farmer was Christian Benner who lived east of Gettysburg.

41. John T. Campbell, letter to the editor of *The National Tribune*, Washington, D.C., September 17, 1908. Campbell's brother was a member of the 4th U.S. Artillery, Battery C and had died of wounds on July 20.

42. Andrew B. Cross, op. cit., pp. 25-26.

43. Jane B. Moore, letter to G.S. Griffin on July 26, printed in the *Lutheran Observer* on August 21, 1863.

44. Frank M. Stoke, letter to his brother written on October 26, 1863. In possession of the Gettysburg College Library.

One Virginia visitor to the field in 1872, Captain Charles Dimmock, reported that, "the trenches in which the dead are buried [where Pickett's men struck the Federal line] were discovered with difficulty, and mainly by the proximity of skeletons which had been ploughed up and now lay strewn about the surface." Dimmock boxed up many of these bones and sent them to Richmond to be buried along with the other remains which had been found by Weaver.

45. E.W. Hutter, "Four Days on the Battlefield of Gettysburg." Article written in the *Lutheran and Missionary* on July 23, 1863.

46. John B. Linn, copy of his diary in the files of the Gettysburg National Military Park Library.

47. Edward A. Bird, copy of his diary in the files of the Gettysburg National Military Park Library.

48. Isaac Morehead, "A Visit to Gettysburg." An article in *The American Magazine and Historical Chronicle*. Vol. 1, No. 2, 1985-86, published by the Clements Library, Ann Arbor, Michigan. Armistead lost four colonels killed or motally wounded on July 3: Hodges, Edmonds, Magruder, and Wade. Pickett lost ten altogether.

Joseph Parker, a college student who walked over the Round Tops on July 21, said:

> . . . but the worst sight that I saw was a Confederate that had not been buried at all, most of his body was decayed, his head was disconnected from his body and on the whole presented a most horrid sight; I covered him with his blanket. . . .

49. Gettysburg *Star and Sentinel*. An article entitled "The Rebel Dead" in the February 2, 1864 issue.

50. Various notes in the author's files; also a conversation with Kathleen G. Harrison on September 9, 1989.
Copy of J.D. Frey's journal loaned by the Larson family and the General Lee's Headquarters Museum.
Copy of Samuel Weaver's Burial Roster at the Gettysburg National Military Park Library.
J.W.C. O'Neal's *Physician's Handbook for 1863-67*, at the Adams County Historical Society.

51. James K.P. Scott, *The Story of the Battle of Gettysburg*. The Telegraph Press, Harrisburg, Pennsylvania, 1927, p. 35.

52. From a copy of "Elliott's Map of the Battlefield of Gettysburg" in the author's files.

53. Rufus B. Weaver, obituary in "The Hahnemannian Institute," Vol. III, No. 2, Hahnemann Medical College, Philadelphia, Pennsylvania, December, 1895.

54. The Hollywood Memorial Association of Richmond's "indebtedness statement" to Rufus B. Weaver (May 7, 1872-July 7, 1873) in the files of the Gettysburg National Military Park Library. It appears that the reason only 3,320 were removed is because Weaver disinterred many of the Southern remains from Union and Confederate former field and general hospital sites. Apparently he did not find all of the graves which were on the battlefield proper. After so many years, many of these graves were long lost or destroyed by the weather, visitation, and poor initial burials.

55. John W. Busey, *These Honored Dead, The Union Casualties at Gettysburg*. Longstreet House, Hightstown, New Jersey, 1988, p. 12. Notes in the "Confederate Bodies Found" file at the Gettysburg National Military Park Library, and discussion with author Roy Frampton.

56. Jacob Hoke, op. cit., p. 172.

57. J. Howard Wert, op. cit., "In the Hospitals of Gettysburg."

58. The names of Confederates buried around Gettysburg and the burial sites they occupied were found in several lists at the Gettysburg National Military Park Library, viz.:

— Dr. J.W.C. O'Neal, "List of Marked Confederates Buried Upon the Battlefield of Gettysburg."

— Dr. J.W.C. O'Neal, "List of Graves of Confederate Soldiers Lying on the Battlefield Still Marked, Taken in May 1866."

— Dr. R.B Weaver, "Papers Listing Confederate Dead Exhumed on the Battlefield of Gettysburg."

— also: "CONFEDERATE DEATHS AND INTERMENTS, GETTYSBURG", RG 94, National Archives and Records Service.

59. J. Howard Wert, "Twas Fifty Years Ago" The Story of the Battle of Gettysburg, #13," Harrisburg *Telegraph*, July, 1913.

60. S.G. Elliott, "Map," op. cit.

61. Sophronia E. Bucklin, op. cit., p. 189.

62. Jacob Hoke, op. cit., p. 172.

63. Decimus et Ultimus Barziza. *The Adventures of a Prisoner of War 1863-4*. Ed. by R.H. Shuffler. University of Texas Press, Austin, 1964, p. 55.

64. Official Records, Vol. 27, pt. 2. See Index in this citation for name of officers or enlisted men mentioned in text.
J.W.C. O'Neal, "Journal" in files of Adams County Historical Society.
J.W. Lokey. *Wounded at Gettysburg*, Confederate Veteran, Vol. 22, 1914.
Samuel Weaver, letter written on December 27, 1865, in Gettysburg National Military Park Library.

65. Andrew Cross, op. cit., p. 26.
Edward Bird, op. cit., p. 10.

66. Georgeanna Woolsey. *Letters of a Family During the War for the Union*, Vol. II. Privately printed, 1899.

67. J.W.C. O'Neal, article in Gettysburg *Compiler*, July 5, 1905.
J.W.C. O'Neal, Physicians Visiting Book, 1863, at Adams County Historical Society.

68. Official Records, Vol. 27, pt. 2.
John N. Opie, *A Rebel Cavalryman with Lee, Stuart and Jackson*, Chicago, 1899.

69. William C. Oates, op. cit., p. 221.

70. Official Records, Vol. 27, pt. 2.
D. Augustus Dickert, op. cit., p. 250.

71. Paul Lentz, article in the May 11, 1986, Concord *Tribune*, Concord, North Carolina.

72. Emily B. Souder. *Leaves from the Battlefield of Gettysburg*. Caxton Press, Philadelphia, Pennsylvania, 1864, p. 34.

73. J.W.C. O'Neal, notes in "Journal" at Adams County Historical Society.

74. George A. Otis, U.S. Surgeon's report to Army Medical Museum.

75. Archie K. Davis. *Boy Colonel of the Confederacy.* . . . The University of North Carolina Press, Chapel Hill, 1985.

76. Wm. N. Wood. *Reminiscences of Big I.* Ed. by B.I. Wiley. McCowat-Mercer Press, Inc., Jackson, Tennessee, 1956, p. 44.
Official Records, Vol. 27, pt. 2.
Robert K. Krick, *Lee's Colonels*. Press of Morningside Bookshop, Dayton, Ohio, 1984. See individual officer as listed.

77. Clarissa F. Jones, article in Philadelphia "North American," June 29, 1913.

78. Abner R. Small. *Road to Richmond*. Ed. by Harold A. Small. University of California Press, Berkeley, California, 1939, p. 107.

79. Jane B. Moore, op. cit.
J. Howard Wert, op. cit., "Twas Fifty Years Ago . . .", #12.

80. Robert K. Krick, op. cit.

Andrew B. Cross, op. cit.

Thomas D. Witherspoon, "Prison Life at Fort McHenry," Southern Historical Society Papers, Vol. VIII, 1880.

Robert E. Lee, letter to General George G. Meade, was at one time in the collection of Ted and Mary Sutphen, Gettysburg, Pennsylvania.

Colonel Alleman was the post commander at the 36th PA militia camp at Gettysburg after the battle.

81. Thomas D. Witherspoon, letter to J.W. Phillips written from Orange Court House, Virginia, January 5, 1864, copy at Gettysburg National Military Park Library.

82. Unknown Confederate officer, article in *The Land We Love*. Hill, Irwin & Co., Charlotte, North Carolina, Vol. II, 1866-67, p. 39.

J.W.C. O'Neal, "Burial List" in files at Gettysburg National Military Park Library.

83. Robert K. Krick, op. cit.

Charles Blacknall, memoir in North Carolina Department of Archives and History, Raleigh, North Carolina.

Gregory A. Coco, op. cit., *A Vast Sea of Misery*. General Iverson was said to have ordered his men into an attack which was destined to fail; he was not present in the attack - and some accused him of being drunk.

84. R.B. Weaver, letter to Dr. J.W.C. O'Neal, February 19, 1887. In 1943 the original was in the possession of J.T. Huddle, Gettysburg, Pennsylvania. Copy in author's files.

85. Gettysburg *Star and Sentinel*, "Notice" dated August 15, 1863.

Dan McGuire, Reston, Virginia. This information in files of McGuire was supplied to author. He is actively seeking material on this officer.

J.W.C. O'Neal, op. cit., "Journal."

86. *Recollections of Gettysburg as Told By Soldiers and Others*. Author unknown, privately published.

Azor H. Nickerson, "Personal Recollections of Two Visits to Gettysburg," *Scribner's Magazine*, New York, 1893.

87. Elizabeth S. Myers, article in San Francisco *Sunday Call*, August 16, 1903.

Elizabeth S. Myers, article in Philadelphia *North American*, July 4, 1909.

Elizabeth S. Myers, article in Chattanooga *News*, February 20, 1913.

88. John E. Dooley. *John Dooley, Confederate Soldier, His War Journal.* Ed. by J.T. Durkin. University of Notre Dame Press, Notre Dame, Wisconsin, 1963, p. 110-112

89. John E. Dooley, op. cit., p. 112.

90. Robert K. Krick, op. cit.
Kathleen G. Harrison and John W. Busey. *Nothing But Glory.* Longstreet House, Hightstown, New Jersey, 1987.
John E. Dooley, op. cit., p. 109.

91. D. Augustus Dickert, op. cit.

92. Robert K. Krick, op. cit.
Kathleen G. Harrison and John W. Busey, op. cit., *Nothing But Glory.*
J. Howard Wert, op. cit., "Twas Fifty Years Ago . . .," #12.
J.W.C. O'Neal, op. cit., "Journal."

93. Official Records, Vol. 27, pt. 2.
J. Howard Wert, op. cit., "Twas Fifty Years Ago . . .," #12.

94. William C. Oates, op. cit., p. 674.

95. John Y. Foster, "Four Days at Gettysburg," Harper's New Monthly Magazine, February, 1864.

96. Hanover Chamber of Commerce. *Encounter at Hanover, Prelude to Gettysburg.* Times & News Publishing Co., Gettysburg, 1962, p. 100.

97. J.W.C. O'Neal, letters to Lucy H. Wood, June 10, 1869, and Joseph W. Southall, August 10, 1869, in files at Gettysburg National Military Park Library.

98. Gettysburg *Star and Sentinel*, article or notice, May 15, 1878.

99. Henry E. Handerson. *Yankee in Gray.* The Press of Western Reserve University, 1962, pp. 62-64.
Information available at the Gettysburg National Military Park Visitor Center's "Museum of the Civil War."

100. LeGrand J. Wilson. *The Confederate Soldier.* Ed. by James W. Silver. Memphis State University Press, Memphis, Tennessee, 1973, p. 121.

Maud Morrow Brown. *The University Greys*. Garrett and Massie, Richmond, Virginia, 1940.

101. Randolph H. McKim. *A Soldier's Recollections*. Zenger Publishing Co., Washington, D.C., 1983, p. 183.

102. LeGrand J. Wilson, op. cit., p. 119.
Thomas D. Witherspoon, op. cit.
Thomas D. Witherspoon, op. cit., letter written to Lieutenant J.W. Phillips.

103. J.B. Polley. *Hood's Texas Brigade*. Press of Morningside Bookshop, Dayton, Ohio, 1976, p. 177.

104. Jane Mitchel, letter to James Mitchel, dated June 10 (no year) in files at Gettysburg National Military Park Library.

105. John W. Busey. *The Last Full Measure*. Longstreet House: Hightstown, New Jersey, 1988, p. xx.
Randolph H. McKim, op. cit., p. 189.
Henry K. Douglas. *I Rode With Stonewall*. University of North Carolina Press: Chapel Hill, 1968, p. 250.
S.G. Elliott, "Map.", op. cit.

106. J.W.C. O'Neal, letter to C.B. Burns, October 5, 1886, in files at Gettysburg National Military Park Library.

107. R.B. Weaver, letter to Dr. J.W.C. O'Neal, October 27, 1886.
J.W.C. O'Neal, "Burial List," at Gettysburg National Military Park Library.
William C. Storrick, "Battlefield Notes," Gettysburg *Compiler*, July 24, 1926.

108. S.G. Elliott, "Map.", op. cit.,
R.B. Weaver, shipment invoices, 1871, at Gettysburg National Military Park Library.
Robert K. Krick, op. cit.
R.B. Weaver, letter to Mrs. R.L. Campbell, dated October 9, 1871, in files of the Gettysburg National Military Park Library.

109. George G. Benedict, op. cit., p. 169.
Joseph W. Muffly. *The Story of Our Regiment*. Kenyon Printing & Manufacturing Company, Des Moines, Iowa, 1904.
William M. Bogg, letter to John B. Bachelder dated May 19, 1882,

"Bachelder Papers" at Gettysburg National Military Park Library.

110. George T. Fleming, article in the Pittsburgh *Gazette Times*, dated November 9, 1913.
One other Gettysburg area youth who accompanied Culp to Virginia with Mr. Hoffman was J.B. Sheffler, who also served in the 2nd Virginia. Both he and Culp were captured in 1862 while on furlough.
Henry K. Douglas, op. cit., p. 251.
John O. Casler. *Four Years in the Stonewall Brigade*. Morningside Bookshop, Dayton, Ohio, 1971, p. 182.

111. "Report of the General Agent of the State of New York . . ." Comstock & Cassidy Printers, Albany, 1864.

112. Robert K. Krick. *Parker's Virginia Battery, C.S.A..* Virginia Book Company, Berryville, Virginia, 1975, p. 163.

113. "McConnellsburg (PA) Skirmish File" at the Gettysburg National Military Park Library.

114. Jacob Hoke. *The Great Invasion*. W.J. Shuey Publisher: Dayton, Ohio. 1887, p. 200.
Imboden's command consisted of the 18th Va. Cav., 62nd Va. Mounted Infantry, McNeil's Va. Partisian Rangers and McClanahan's Va. Battery.

115. R.B. Weaver, "Papers Listing Confederate Remains Exhumed on the Battlefield of Gettysburg . . ." Records of the Hollywood Memorial Association at Gettysburg National Military Park Library. Note of grave marker found by Weaver. Engraved plaque on the headboard of the grave of Private Radford G. Gunn 17th Mississippi Infantry

116. John H. Brinton. *Personal Memoirs of* . . . . Neale Publishing Company, New York, 1914, p. 245.

117. Sophronia E. Bucklin, op. cit., p. 189.

118. Leander Warren. *My Recollections* . . . . Privately printed in Gettysburg.

119. Benjamin H. Child, "From Fredericksburg to Gettysburg," Personal Narratives, Rhode Island Soldiers and Sailors Historical Society, 5, #4.

120. John W. Busey, op. cit., p. xviii.

121. Richard Irby. *Historical Sketch of the Nottoway Grays* .... J.W. Fergusson & Sons, Richmond, Virginia, 1878, p. 29.

122. These articles were found in a file, "Confederate Bodies Found" in the Gettysburg National Military Park Library.

Index

For additional burial sites and soldiers' names and regiments not listed in this index, see Part III and Appendices C and D.

189

Gregory A. Coco, born in 1946, grew up in Mansura, Avoyelles Parish, Louisiana. He graduated from the University of Southwestern Louisiana in 1972 with a B.A. degree in history. From 1967 to 1969, Coco served in the U.S. Army, including a tour in Vietnam, where as an infantryman he was wounded twice. Since his return to civilian life, Coco has worked as a Louisiana state trooper, and as a park ranger, historian, maintenance worker, and licensed battlefield guide at the Gettysburg National Military Park.

Other books by the author:
Through Blood and Fire: The Civil War Letters of Charles J. Mills (1981); *On The Bloodstained Field* (1987); *A Vast Sea of Misery: A History and Guide to the Union and Confederate Field Hospitals at Gettysburg* (1988); *On The Bloodstained Field II* (1989); and *Recollections of a Texas Colonel at Gettysburg* (1990).

William H. Ridinger was born in Gettysburg, Pennsylvania in 1917. He attended Gettysburg College, Columbia University, and New York University where he earned degrees in history and education. Dr. Ridinger, after a long and distinguished career as an educator, has "retired" to the Gettysburg area and is a licensed battlefield guide and lecturer. When not conducting seminars, tours, and symposiums on the Civil War, Bill enjoys tennis, hiking, and camping.

Daniel E. Fuhrman was born in 1961, in Hanover, Pennsylvania, where he now lives with his wife Cynthia S. Roller and their new son Bryce. He graduated from Southwestern High School in 1979, and then studied drafting and design for three years at the Electronics Institute of Harrisburg. Dan is currently employed as a draftsman by P.H. Glatfelter Company of Spring Grove, Pennsylvania. Besides his love of art, he is an avid outdoor enthusiast enjoying sports such as running, biking and racewalking. Fuhrman has now entered college to further his career in art, design and mechanical drawing.

John S. Heiser was born and raised in Raleigh, North Carolina. He has had an interest in the Civil War since the age of six, and continuing this interest, John received his degree in American History from Western Carolina University. An employee of the National Park Service since 1978, in his spare time he has also contributed illustrations and maps for other works, including the three volumes of *The Vicksburg Campaign* by Edwin Bearss. John is married to Carmen Johnson and they reside in Gettysburg.

THOMAS PUBLICATIONS publishes books about the American Colonial era, the Revolutionary War, the Civil War, and other important topics. For a complete list of titles, please write to:

THOMAS PUBLICATIONS
P. O. Box 3031
Gettysburg, PA 17325